This series offers the concerned reader basic guidelines and *practical* applications of religion for today's world. Although decidedly Christian in focus and emphasis, the series embraces all denominations and modes of Bible-based belief relevant to our lives today. All volumes in the Steeple series are originals, freshly written to provide a fresh perspective on current—and yet timeless—human dilemmas. This is a series for our times. Among the books in the series:.

Woman in Despair: A Christian Guide to Self-Repair
Elizabeth Rice Handford

A Spiritual Handbook for Women
Dandi Daley Knorr

How to Read the Bible
James Fischer

Bible Solutions to Problems of Daily Living
James W. Steele

In the World but Not of It: A Guide to Spirituality in Your Life
Stuart B. Litvak and Norma Burba

A Book of Devotions for Today's Woman
Frances Carroll

Temptation: How Christians Can Deal with It
Frances Carroll

With God on Your Side: A Guide to Finding Self-Worth through Total Faith
Doug Manning

Help in Ages Past, Hope for Years to Come: Daily Devotions from the Old Testament
Robert L Cate

A Daily Key for Today's Christians: 365 Key Texts of the New Testament
William E. Bowles

Walking in the Garden: Inner Peace from the Flowers of God
Paula Connor

How to Bring up Children in the Catholic Faith
Carol and David Powell

Sex in the Bible: An Introduction to What the Scriptures Teach Us About Sexuality
Michael R. Cosby

How to Talk with God Every Day of the Year: A Book of Devotions for Twelve Positive Months
Frances Hunter

God's Conditions for Prosperity: How to Earn the Rewards of Christian Living
Charles Hunter

Pilgrimages: A Guide to the Holy Places of Europe for Today's Traveler
Paul Lambourne Higgins

Journey into the Light: Lessons of Pain and Joy to Renew Your Energy and Strengthen Your Faith
Dorris Blough Murdock

WILLIAM E. BOWLES has been the minister of Central Christian Church in Arkansas City, Kansas, since 1973. He developed a popular booklet, *Let the Bible Be Your Guide*, and has written numerous articles for religious journals and Bible study guides.

A DAILY KEY FOR TODAY'S CHRISTIANS

365 KEY TEXTS OF THE NEW TESTAMENT

William E. Bowles

PRENTICE-HALL, INC.
Englewood Cliffs, N.J. 07632

Library of Congress Cataloging in Publication Data

Bowles, William E.
A daily key for today's Christians.
(Steeple books)
A Spectrum Book.
Includes index.
1. Devotional calendars. I. Bible. N.T. English.
Selections. 1984. II. Title. III. Series.
BS391.2.B69 1984 242'.2 83-21290
ISBN 0-13-196113-6
ISBN 0-13-196105-5 (pbk.)

This book is available at a special discount when ordered in bulk quantities. Contact Prentice-Hall, Inc., General Publishing Division, Special Sales, Englewood Cliffs, New Jersey 07632.

A SPECTRUM BOOK

Printed in the United States of America

1 2 3 4 5 6 7 8 9 10

ISBN 0-13-196105-5 {PBK.}

ISBN 0-13-196113-6

Editorial/production supervision by Claudia Citarella
Cover design by Hal Siegel
Manufacturing buyer: Ed Ellis

PRENTICE-HALL INTERNATIONAL, INC., *London*
PRENTICE-HALL OF AUSTRALIA PTY. LIMITED, *Sydney*
PRENTICE-HALL OF CANADA, INC., *Toronto*
PRENTICE-HALL OF INDIA PRIVATE LIMITED, *New Delhi*
PRENTICE-HALL OF JAPAN, INC., *Tokyo*
PRENTICE-HALL OF SOUTHEAST ASIA PTE. LTD., *Singapore*
WHITEHALL BOOKS LIMITED, *Wellington, New Zealand*
EDITORA PRENTICE-HALL DO BRASIL, LTD., Rio de Janeiro

This book is dedicated to many friends:

- — a loving family and relatives
- — Christian laity who have taught me how to minister
- — dedicated college, seminary, and graduate school professors
- — colleague pastors in various denominations of Christianity whose lives have helped keep me growing through the years in the practical wisdom of the New Testament

CONTENTS

PREFACE

HOW DID THIS BOOK BEGIN?

Let me explain what inspired *A Daily Key for Today's Christians: 365 Key Texts of the New Testament* as a contemporary catalyst for Christian devotion. One evening our teenage daughter, Julie, was looking for a good Scripture to relate to a friend in dealing with a problem they were both facing. I helped her find a relevant Scripture and thought, "How can I help Julie make the teachings of the New Testament a practical part of her Christian living?" I also thought of my brother, John, a successful chemical engineer and a dedicated Christian. I thought, "How can the typical busy, responsible Christian find time to stay in touch with the essential life-giving spiritual inspirations of Holy Scripture?" Through the years fellow Christians and members of my own family have kept challenging me in the practical use of the New Testament. They would ask questions such as "What are some favorite Scriptures worth memorizing?" "What is the point of these particular verses?" "What are the Scriptures asking us to do?" "How can the Scriptures help us to pray?"

As a pastor, I have been concerned for many years about two divergent but deficient expressions of the Christian faith. On the one hand, great numbers of church members apparently have a sensible understanding of the Christian faith but seem helpless in sharing any specific Scriptures with others. On the other hand, some overzealous Christians quote certain Scriptures but demonstrate they do not really know the overall message and spirit of the New Testament.

A Daily Key for Today's Christians encourages another stance, that of the necessity of grounding personal and corporate Christianity—whether one leans toward the liberal or the conservative—on the solid foundation of the Bible. Both Church history and individual Christian experience have verified that a balanced and enthusiastic Christian faith can only emerge from a comprehensive understanding of Scripture.

WHO WILL THIS BOOK HELP?

This book is a contemporary catalyst for Christian devotion for new Christians, searching Christians, and growing Christians.

- — *New Christians* will find in it the central themes and message of the entire New Testament without getting bogged down in the more difficult passages.
- — *Searching Christians*, who have been in the Church for some time and who have never fully understood what the Bible is all about, will find in this book a clarification of the essential teachings and beliefs of Christianity.
- — *Growing Christians*, who already know a great deal about the New Testament, will find this book a challenge to review and reflect on familiar texts that together relate the drama of God's salvation and our Christian mission.

A Daily Key for Today's Christians will be especially useful for *busy Christians*, who sometimes neglect the springs of inspiration in the Scripture for Christian confidence and Christian action.

This book can be read from day to day beginning any time of the year. The key ideas after each day's reading will spark your own thinking on the meaning and application of the New Testament for today. The suggested action step for each day will encourage you to follow through on the inspirations you have received from the Scripture. Prayer will take on a new integrity when you link it to constructive action. The one-sentence prayers can be an opportunity for making a new discovery in genuine conversational prayer. Consider it a primer in each day's practice of the presence of God.

A Daily Key for Today's Christians is especially prepared for individual and family use, but it can also serve as a help for fellowship groups, congregational Bible reading, and spiritual life development. It would certainly enhance the dialogue of preaching if the leadership of a congregation, a covenant group, or an entire parish or congregation chose to read *A*

Daily Key for Today's Christians in concert with a year of preaching, prayer, and practice of the total message of the New Testament. Such an adventure would surely do much to infuse a balanced biblical awareness and new depth of faith into the minds of today's church members.

The New Testament is an exciting and inspiring source of spiritual and practical wisdom. Today one of the happy surprises for many church members and nonchurch members is that the New Testament is not for Bible scholars only. It was written for persons of all professions and in all walks of life. If one spends time with only critical literary and historical questions, many of the great riches of the Bible will be overlooked. *A Daily Key for Today's Christians* is a way to move into a refreshing discovery or rediscovery of the relevance of the New Testament to our contemporary life.

INTRODUCTION

THE BASIS OF SELECTING KEY TEXTS

In contrast to many summaries of Scriptures, *A Daily Key for Today's Christians* is not simply an anthology of Scriptures divided into themes or literary styles. Nor is it a collection of ethical teachings that leaves out statements of the essentials of the Christian faith. Rather, the message of the whole New Testament is included—basic beliefs and instructions for living.

This collection of the key texts of the New Testament is the product of years of scholarly study of the Bible and work with mature Christians who know their Bible well. The compiler has been on guard lest, for special theological reasons of his own, major Biblical beliefs and doctrines, certain sections, or various types of literature of the New Testament be unconsciously omitted. Every effort has been made to include the major texts and portions of the great chapters of the New Testament as would be recognized by capable Christian pastors and teachers. And even though these selections are only from the New Testament, the influence of the Hebraic faith of the Old Testament is evident throughout.

The following factors helped determine the choice of the 365 core texts of the New Testament to be read over a period of one year:

1. These are the favorite Scriptures of the Church.
2. These are texts representative of the total message of the New Testament.

3. There are many concise memorable portions that can be of assistance in daily Christian living and for Christian witnessing; no quotation is broken up by omission of middle verses.
4. There is at least one selection from every New Testament book, recognizing their relative differences in number of chapters; all selections other than the Gospels are listed in the order in which they appear by books and chapters in the New Testament.
5. There are selections from each of the four Gospels including representative teachings, parables, miracles, and dialogues; the Gospel texts are listed in sequence according to the traditionally accepted outline of the life and ministry of Jesus.

AN INVITATION TO YOU

Never before have we had access to so many good modern translations of the New Testament that are finding respect by ecumenical and evangelical Christians. The Revised Standard Version (Common Bible),* which has gained widespread acceptance in Protestant and Catholic churches, is the basic text used in this book. You may have another favorite translation of the New Testament which you wish to use along with this book. Some of the other very popular modern translations today are the New International Version, New American Bible, Good News for Modern Man, New English Bible, New American Standard Bible, J.B. Phillips Translation, Jerusalem Bible, Living Bible, and The New King James Bible. All these offer additional inspirations and insights for enthusiastic explorers and Christian teachers.

A Daily Key for Today's Christians invites you to engage in a personal dialogue with the Word of God through the New Testament. The Word of God in Scripture is God's personal Word for helping you encounter your present life situations, for asking you for a personal response of obedience to the way of Christ, and for leading you to engage in a personal dialogue with others in the Spirit. *A Daily Key for Today's Christians* offers you a key in the search for truth, a key to the Christian experience of human relationships, and a key to deeper communion with God.

*The Scripture quotations in this publication are from the Revised Standard Version (Common Bible), copyrighted © 1973 by the Division of Christian Education of the National Council of the Churches of Christ of the U.S.A. and are used by permission.

A DAILY KEY FOR TODAY'S CHRISTIANS

1 IN THE BEGINNING

In the beginning was the Word, and the Word was with God, and the Word was God. He was in the beginning with God; all things were made through him, and without him was not anything made that was made. In him was life, and the life was the light of men. The light shines in the darkness, and the darkness has not overcome it. (*John 1:1–5*)

Key Ideas: The creative Word
The life-giving Word
The light-giving Word

Action Step: Speak or write of your love for someone; then do something to communicate and demonstrate the meaning of your words.

Prayer: Lord, I will rejoice today in Your holy and human Word for our world.

2 THE WORD BECAME FLESH

The true light that enlightens every man was coming into the world. He was in the world, and the world was made through him, yet the world knew him not. He came to his own home, and his own people received him not. But to all who received him, who believed in his name, he gave power to become children of God; who were born, not of blood nor of the will of the flesh nor of the will of man, but of God. And the Word became flesh and dwelt among us, full of grace and truth; we have beheld his glory, glory as of the only Son from the Father. (John bore witness to him, and cried, "This was he of whom I said, 'He who comes after me ranks before me, for he was before me.' ") And from his fulness have we all received, grace upon grace. For the law was given through Moses; grace and truth came through Jesus Christ. (*John 1:9–17*)

Key Ideas: The Bringer of new life
God's personal and human presence
A new stage in human existence

Action Step: Correspond with a Christian missionary, international or fraternal worker, or Christian leader of another country; express your appreciation to them and your conviction that Jesus is God's Word, and that the Word is adequate for the whole world.

Prayer: I know today, Lord, that whatever else I am, I belong to You as a "child of God."

3 THE MIRACULOUS BIRTH

Now the birth of Jesus Christ took place in this way. When his mother Mary had been betrothed to Joseph, before they came together she was found to be with child of the Holy Spirit; and her husband Joseph, being a just man and unwilling to put her to shame, resolved to divorce her quietly. But as he considered this, behold, an angel of the Lord appeared to him in a dream, saying, "Joseph, son of David, do not fear to take Mary your wife, for that which is conceived in her is of the Holy Spirit; she will bear a son, and you shall call his name Jesus, for he will save his people from their sins." All this took place to fulfil what the Lord had spoken by the prophet:

> Behold a virgin shall conceive and bear a son, and his name shall be called Emmanu-el

(which means, God with us). (*Matthew 1:18–23*)

Key Ideas: A Child of the Holy Spirit

Call Him *Jesus, the Savior*
He is called *God with Us*

Action Step: Take a walk through a park or find a quiet place away from distractions or interruptions; make time to be alone with God.

Prayer: Lord, in the silences of today I will be listening closely for Your words of guidance in my particular situation.

4 THE SAVIOR BORN

In those days a decree went out from Caesar Augustus that all the world should be enrolled. This was the first enrollment, when Quirini-us was governor of Syria. And all went to be enrolled, each to his own city. And Joseph also went up from Galilee, from the city of Nazareth, to Judea, to the city of David, which is called Bethlehem, because he was of the house and lineage of David, to be enrolled with Mary, his betrothed, who was with child. And while they were there, the time came for her to be delivered. And she gave birth to her first-born son and wrapped him in swaddling cloths, and laid him in a manger, because there was no place for them in the inn. (*Luke 2:1–7*)

Key Ideas: Ruler of the Roman Empire
Jesus' kingly ancestry
The Messiah was born in a manger

Action Step: Look at the available housing in your community; support fair, more available, and better housing for the total population.

Prayer: Surely, Lord, today I dare not demand a life void of adversity since I know what Your only Son endured.

5 THE PRINCE OF PEACE

And in that region there were shepherds out in the field, keeping watch over their flock by night. And an angel of the Lord appeared to them, and the glory of the Lord shone around them, and they were filled with fear. And the angel said to them, "Be not afraid; for behold, I bring you good news of a great joy which will come to all the people; for to you is born this day in the city of David a Savior, who is Christ the Lord. And this will be a sign for you: you will find a babe wrapped in swaddling cloths and lying in a manger." And suddenly there was with the angel a multitude of the heavenly host praising God and saying,

> Glory to God in the highest, and on earth peace among men with whom he is pleased!

(*Luke 2:8–14*)

Key Ideas: Surprised by angels
Where Christ was born
God's way to peace

Action Step: Offer your support to the agencies of peace; don't wait for perfect organizations before getting involved; let Christ work through you now.

Prayer: Lord, I want to be ready to hear and follow the angels of hope who sing in our world today.

6 THE WISE MEN

Then Herod summoned the wise men secretly and ascertained from them what time the star appeared; and he sent them to Bethlehem, saying, "Go and search diligently for the child, and when you have found him bring me word, that I too may come and worship him." When they had heard the king they went their way; and lo, the star which they had seen in the East went before them, till it came to rest over the place where the child was. When they saw the star, they rejoiced exceedingly with great joy; and going into the house they saw the child with Mary his mother, and they fell down and worshiped him. Then, opening their treasures, they offered him gifts, gold and frankincense and myrrh. And being warned in a dream not to return to Herod, they departed to their own country by another way. (*Matthew 2:7–12*)

Key Ideas: The Child who threatened a king
Search for a star
Gifts for God's new King

Action Step: Gladden the heart of some children with some significant gift or attention that lets them know they really count in this big world.

Prayer: I marvel today, Lord, over the mystery of Your providential leading alongside our human decisions and choices.

7 THE BOYHOOD OF JESUS

Now his parents went to Jerusalem every year at the feast of the Passover. And when he was twelve years old, they went up according to custom; and when the feast was ended, as they were returning, the boy Jesus stayed behind in Jerusalem. His parents did not know it, but supposing him to be in the company they went a day's journey, and they sought him among their kinsfolk and acquaintances; and when they did not find him, they returned to Jerusalem, seeking him. After three days they found him in the temple, sitting among the teachers, listening to them and asking them questions; and all who heard him were amazed at his understanding and his answers. And when they saw him they were astonished; and his mother said to him, "Son, why have you treated us so? Behold, your father and I have been looking for you anxiously." And he said to them, "How is it that you sought me? Did you not know that I must be in my Father's house?" And they did not understand the saying which he spoke to them. And he went down with them and came to Nazareth, and was obedient to them; and his mother kept all these things in her heart. And Jesus increased in wisdom and in stature, and in favor with God and man. (*Luke 2:41–52*)

Key Ideas: A family festival of faith
The dialogue of religious education
The healthy growth of Jesus

Action Step: Establish with your family a festival of faith in connection with one of the significant days of the Church year.

Prayer: Lord, lead me today toward the "well-rounded life" but always with the courage to be singularly committed to You.

8 JOHN'S WITNESS

As the people were in expectation, and all men questioned in their hearts concerning John, whether perhaps he were the Christ, John answered them all, "I baptize you with water; but he who is mightier than I is coming, the thong of whose sandals I am not worthy to untie; he will baptize you with the Holy Spirit and with fire. His winnowing fork is in his hand, to clear his threshing floor, and to gather the wheat into his granary, but the chaff he will burn with unquenchable fire." (*Luke 3:15–17*)

Key Ideas: Longing for the Messiah
Hopes for the Holy Spirit
A harvest is impending

Action Step: As you read through the Gospel reports about Jesus make notes on how He demonstrated He was the Christ sent from God.

Prayer: Lord, I hope to live today with the strong assurance that what You have purposed for this world in Christ will be accomplished.

9 THE BAPTISM OF JESUS

Then Jesus came from Galilee to the Jordan to John, to be baptized by him. John would have prevented him, saying, "I need to be baptized by you, and do you come to me?" But Jesus answered him, "Let it be so now; for thus it is fitting for us to fulfil all righteousness." Then he consented. And when Jesus was baptized, he went up immediately from the water, and behold, the heavens were opened and he saw the Spirit of God descending like a dove, and alighting on him; and lo, a voice from heaven, saying, "This is my beloved Son, with whom I am well pleased." (*Matthew 3:13–17*)

Key Ideas: Baptized with sinners
Baptized by the Spirit
Baptized for mission

Action Step: Ask a person who has shown some interest in the Church if he or she has ever considered being baptized; you may be the one person to help answer any questions he or she may have.

Prayer: Lord, use me today, all of me that You can, in Your service.

10 CHOICES BEFORE JESUS

Then Jesus was led up by the Spirit into the wilderness to be tempted by the devil. And he fasted forty days and forty nights, and afterward he was hungry. And the tempter came and said to him, "If you are the Son of God, command these stones to become loaves of bread." But he answered, "It is written, 'Man shall not live by bread alone, but by every word that proceeds from the mouth of God.' " Then the devil took him to the holy city, and set him on the pinnacle of the temple, and said to him, "If you are the Son of God, throw yourself down; for it is written, 'He will give his angels charge of you,' and 'On their hands they will bear you up, lest you strike your foot against a stone.' " Jesus said to him, "Again it is written, 'You shall not tempt the Lord your God.' " Again, the devil took him to a very high mountain, and showed him all the kingdoms of the world and the glory of them; and he said to him, "All these I will give you, if you will fall down and worship me." Then Jesus said to him, "Begone, Satan! for it is written, 'You shall worship the Lord your God and him only shall you serve.' " Then the devil left him, and behold, angels came and ministered to him." (*Matthew 4:1–11*)

Key Ideas: The temptation of magic
The temptation of special privileges
The temptation of "success"

Action Step: Turn to the Old Testament Scriptures and selectively draw from it spiritual resources the way Jesus did; mark and memorize several of these great texts.

Prayer: I need Your wisdom, Lord, to see the alternatives for good or evil in the way I utilize my abilities and opportunities today.

11 BEING BORN ANEW

Now there was a man of the Pharisees, named Nicodemus, a ruler of the Jews. This man came to Jesus by night and said to him, "Rabbi, we know that you are a teacher come from God; for no one can do these signs that you do, unless God is with him." Jesus answered him, "Truly, truly, I say to you, unless one is born anew, he cannot see the kingdom of God." Nicodemus said to him, "How can a man be born when he is old? Can he enter a second time into his mother's womb and be born?" Jesus answered, "Truly, truly, I say to you, unless one is born of water and the Spirit, he cannot enter the kingdom of God. That which is born of the flesh is flesh, and that which is born of the Spirit is spirit. Do not marvel that I said to you, 'You must be born anew.' The wind blows where it wills, and you hear the sound of it, but you do not know whence it comes or whither it goes; so it is with every one who is born of the Spirit." (*John 3:1–8*)

Key Ideas: The unavoidable truth about Jesus
The possibility of a second birth
The necessity of the birth by the Spirit

Action Step: Try to describe to someone what life is like when you move from a strictly animal view of life to a higher spiritual plane.

Prayer: Lord, free me today from analysis and debate that are only a dodge from my own need for change and growth.

12 THE GOLDEN TEXT

For God so loved the world that he gave his only Son, that whoever believes in him should not perish but have eternal life. For God sent the Son into the world, not to condemn the world, but that the world might be saved through him. He who believes in him is not condemned; he who does not believe is condemned already, because he has not believed in the name of the only Son of God. And this is the judgment, that the light has come into the world, and men loved darkness rather than light, because their deeds were evil. For every one who does evil hates the light, and does not come to the light, lest his deeds should be exposed. But he who does what is true comes to the light, that it may be clearly seen that his deeds have been wrought in God. (*John 3:16–21*)

Key Ideas: The salvaging love of God
The believing relationship
The choice is ours

Action Step: Memorize the "golden text" of the Bible; then in your own words paraphrase it in several different ways.

Prayer: Lord, I am captivated today by the very heart of Your being, Your unrelenting, self-giving love for the whole human race.

13 THE WATER OF LIFE

The woman said to him, "Sir, you have nothing to draw with, and the well is deep; where do you get that living water? Are you greater than our father Jacob, who gave us the well, and drank from it himself, and his sons, and his cattle?" Jesus said to her, "Every one who drinks of this water will thirst again, but whoever drinks of the water that I shall give him will never thirst; the water that I shall give him will become in him a spring of water welling up to eternal life." The woman said to him, "Sir, give me this water, that I may not thirst, nor come here to draw." Jesus said to her, "Go, call your husband, and come here." The woman answered him, "I have no husband." Jesus said to her, "You are right in saying, 'I have no husband'; for you have had five husbands, and he whom you now have is not your husband; this you said truly." The woman said to him, "Sir, I perceive that you are a prophet. Our fathers worshiped on this mountain; and you say that in Jerusalem is the place where men ought to worship." Jesus said to her, "Woman, believe me, the hour is coming when neither on this mountain nor in Jerusalem will you worship the Father. You worship what you do not know; we worship what we know, for salvation is from the Jews. But the hour is coming, and now is, when the true worshipers will worship the Father in spirit and truth, for such the Father seeks to worship him. God is spirit, and those who worship him must worship in spirit and truth." (*John 4:11–24*)

Key Ideas: The water of a different kind
The penetrating wisdom of Jesus
The universalizing heart of worship

Action Step: Tell your church's worship leaders what you think are the most uplifting and authentic features of your church's worship.

Prayer: Lord, today I celebrate the invitation from You to drink deeply of that life which has eternal qualities.

14 THE FIRST EVANGEL

And he came to Nazareth, where he had been brought up; and he went to the synagogue, as his custom was, on the sabbath day. And he stood up to read; and there was given to him the book of the prophet Isaiah. He opened the book, and found the place where it was written,

> The Spirit of the Lord is upon me, because he has anointed me to preach good news to the poor. He has sent me to proclaim release to the captives and recovering of sight to the blind, to set at liberty those who are oppressed, to proclaim the acceptable year of the Lord.

And he closed the book, and gave it back to the attendant, and sat down; and the eyes of all in the synagogue were fixed on him. And he began to say to them, "Today this scripture has been fulfilled in your hearing." (*Luke 4:16–21*)

Key Ideas: Scripture in worship

Manifesto of the Messiah
The Word of God for us

Action Step: Make your contribution toward developing your church's mission to encompass Jesus' understanding of the Evangel (Good News) from God.

Prayer: Lord, liberty from external oppression is essential, but I cannot rest today until I can experience for myself and lead others to freedom of the soul.

15 LESSON IN A BOAT

Getting into one of the boats, which was Simon's, he asked him to put out a little from the land. And he sat down and taught the people from the boat. And when he had ceased speaking, he said to Simon, "Put out into the deep and let down your nets for a catch." And Simon answered, "Master, we toiled all night and took nothing! But at your word I will let down the nets." And when they had done this, they enclosed a great shoal of fish; and as their nets were breaking, they beckoned to their partners in the other boat to come and help them. And they came and filled both the boats, so that they began to sink. But when Simon Peter saw it, he fell down at Jesus' knees, saying, "Depart from me, for I am a sinful man, O Lord." For he was astonished, and all that were with him, at the catch of fish which they had taken; and so also were James and John, sons of Zebedee, who were partners with Simon. And Jesus said to Simon, "Do not be afraid; henceforth you will be catching men." And when they had brought their boats to land, they left everything and followed him. (*Luke 5:3–11*)

Key Ideas: A parable of trying again
Doubting can be faithlessness
Creative evangelism

Action Step: Look for and seek to encourage the hidden ability in persons who are important to you and who are within your reach.

Prayer: I will not hold back, Lord, when I hear Your invitation today to move out beyond safe and sure routines of living.

And in the synagogue there was a man who had the spirit of an unclean demon; and he cried out with a loud voice, "Ah! What have you to do with us, Jesus of Nazareth? Have you come to destroy us? I know who you are, the Holy One of God." But Jesus rebuked him, saying, "Be silent, and come out of him!" And when the demon had thrown him down in the midst, he came out of him, having done him no harm. And they were all amazed and said to one another, "What is this word? For with authority and power he commands the unclean spirits, and they come out." (*Luke 4:33–36*)

Key Ideas: Disturbing the demons
Casting out demons
Physician of the soul

Action Step: Meet others today at the point and level of their need rather than of your own interest alone.

Prayer: Lord, today I will face my world of mental and emotional stress with realism and hope.

17 A DAY WITH JESUS

And in the morning, a great while before day, he rose and went out to a lonely place, and there he prayed. And Simon and those who were with him pursued him, and they found him and said to him, "Every one is searching for you." And he said to them, "Let us go on to the next towns, that I may preach there also; for that is why I came out." And he went throughout all Galilee, preaching in their synagogues and casting out demons. (*Mark 1:35–39*)

Key Ideas: The morning meeting with God
The demands of the people
The urgency of Jesus' preaching

Action Step: Make time for moments in your busy day to collect your thoughts; listen for the will of God in your daily schedule.

Prayer: Lord, I need Your wisdom today in working out a balance in the rhythm of my work, refreshment, and rest.

And they came, bringing to him a paralytic carried by four men. And when they could not get near him because of the crowd, they removed the roof above him; and when they had made an opening, they let down the pallet on which the paralytic lay. And when Jesus saw their faith, he said to the paralytic, "My son, your sins are forgiven." Now some of the scribes were sitting there, questioning in their hearts, "Why does this man speak thus? It is blasphemy! Who can forgive sins but God alone?" And immediately Jesus, perceiving in his spirit that they thus questioned within themselves, said to them, "Why do you question thus in your hearts? Which is easier, to say to the paralytic, 'Your sins are forgiven'; or to say, 'Rise, take up your pallet and walk'? But that you may know that the Son of man has authority on earth to forgive sins"—he said to the paralytic—"I say to you, rise, take up your pallet and go home." And he rose, and immediately took up the pallet and went out before them all; so that they were all amazed and glorified God, saying, "We never saw anything like this!" (*Mark 2:3–12*)

Key Ideas: Finding a way to help
Holding out hope to another
God's special healing agent

Action Step: Visit a friend impaired by a physical or spiritual paralysis who is learning to walk and cope with life again; commend his or her courage.

Prayer: Use me today, Lord, in Your ministry of healing for the spirit as well as for the body.

19 THE GREAT PHYSICIAN

And as he sat at table in the house, behold, many tax collectors and sinners came and sat down with Jesus and his disciples. And when the Pharisees saw this, they said to his disciples, "Why does your teacher eat with tax collectors and sinners?" But when he heard it, he said, "Those who are well have no need of a physician, but those who are sick. Go and learn what this means, 'I desire mercy, and not sacrifice.' For I came not to call the righteous, but sinners." Then the disciples of John came to him, saying, "Why do we and the Pharisees fast, but your disciples do not fast?" And Jesus said to them, "Can the wedding guests mourn as long as the bridegroom is with them? The days will come, when the bridegroom is taken away from them, and then they will fast. And no one puts a piece of unshrunk cloth on an old garment, for the patch tears away from the garment, and a worse tear is made. Neither is new wine put into old wineskins; if it is, the skins burst, and the wine is spilled, and the skins are destroyed; but new wine is put into fresh wineskins, and so both are preserved." (*Matthew 9:10–17*)

Key Ideas: Widening associations of concern
Seeking out the spiritually sick
New wine and new ways

Action Step: Keep right on greeting and courteously associating at school or work with persons who are bothered by their own behavior and conscience; you may be a mirror of the good which they are struggling to imitate.

Prayer: Lord, I want to sit next to people today who need help in order to inspire them with the contagion of a healthy faith and life.

20 LIKE FATHER, LIKE SON

Jesus said to them, "Truly, truly, I say to you, the Son can do nothing of his own accord, but only what he sees the Father doing; for whatever he does, that the Son does likewise. For the Father loves the Son, and shows him all that he himself is doing; and greater works than these will he show him, that you may marvel. For as the Father raises the dead and gives them life, so also the Son gives life to whom he will. The Father judges no one, but has given all judgment to the Son, that all may honor the Son, even as they honor the Father. He who does not honor the Son does not honor the Father who sent him. Truly, truly, I say to you, he who hears my word and believes him who sent me, has eternal life; he does not come into judgment, but has passed from death to life." (*John 5:19–24*)

Key Ideas: Source of the Son's power
Source of the Son's inspiration
Source of the Son's authority

Action Step: Look around in our society and see what God is doing to bring about His justice, love, and goodness in the world; in some specific way join in God's action.

Prayer: Lord, I am grateful today that You are giving me life with eternal quality through fellowship with Your Son.

21 CHRIST IN SCRIPTURE

"And the Father who sent me has himself borne witness to me. His voice you have never heard, his form you have never seen; and you do not have his word abiding in you, for you do not believe him whom he has sent. You search the scriptures, because you think that in them you have eternal life; and it is they that bear witness to me; yet you refuse to come to me that you may have life. I do not receive glory from men. But I know that you have not the love of God within you. I have come in my Father's name, and you do not receive me; if another comes in his own name, him you will receive. How can you believe, who receive glory from one another and do not seek the glory that comes from the only God?" (*John 5:37–44*)

Key Ideas: The personal witness to God
The scriptural witness to Jesus
God's glory and our glory

Action Step: Approach the reading of Scripture with as much awareness of your biases as possible; ask yourself, "Is there something in this text I may not want to confront because it may question my attitudes or situation in life?"

Prayer: Free me today, Lord, to do the needed tasks that are Your will, regardless of whether I am noticed by others or not.

22 PERSONS ARE PRIMARY

One sabbath he was going through the grainfields; and as they made their way his disciples began to pluck heads of grain. And the Pharisees said to him, "Look, why are they doing what is not lawful on the sabbath?" And he said to them, "Have you never read what David did, when he was in need and was hungry, he and those who were with him: how he entered the house of God, when Abiathar was high priest, and ate the bread of the Presence, which it is not lawful for any but the priests to eat, and also gave it to those who were with him?" And he said to them, "The sabbath was made for man, not man for the sabbath; so the Son of man is lord even of the sabbath." (*Mark 2:23–28*)

Key Ideas: Breaking the letter of the law
Recovering forgotten history
The Spirit of the sabbath

Action Step: Consider your schedule of typical Sunday activities; plan for worship as well as for times of relaxation for yourself and your entire family.

Prayer: Looking today, Lord, at the week ahead I am aiming at a weekend that I can spend creatively as a Christian.

23 BLESSED ATTITUDES

"Blessed are the poor in spirit, for theirs is the kingdom of heaven. Blessed are those who mourn, for they shall be comforted. Blessed are the meek, for they shall inherit the earth. Blessed are those who hunger and thirst for righteousness, for they shall be satisfied. Blessed are the merciful, for they shall obtain mercy. Blessed are the pure in heart, for they shall see God. Blessed are the peacemakers, for they shall be called sons of God. Blessed are those who are persecuted for righteousness' sake, for theirs is the kingdom of heaven." (*Matthew 5:3–10*)

Key Ideas: The holy way is a happy way
Attitudes that Jesus praised
Rewards are spiritual consequences

Action Step: Welcome anyone into your circle of associations who feels a need for spiritual growth or who has a conscience of compassion for hurting humanity.

Prayer: Lord, show me the secret today of fulfillment in the adventurous life toward holiness and helping others.

24 SOMETHING EXTRA

"You are the salt of the earth; but if salt has lost its taste, how shall its saltness be restored? It is no longer good for anything except to be thrown out and trodden under foot by men. You are the light of the world. A city set on a hill cannot be hid. Nor do men light a lamp and put it under a bushel, but on a stand, and it gives light to all in the house. Let your light so shine before men, that they may see your good works and give glory to your Father who is in heaven." (*Matthew 5:13–16*)

Key Ideas: Bright Christians
Overcoming false modesty
Good for something

Action Step: Study the face of Jesus in some of the great art of the past and present; consider how Jesus allowed God's light to shine through His personality.

Prayer: Lord, reveal Your radiance through me today.

25 FULFILLING THE LAW

"Think not that I have come to abolish the law and the prophets; I have come not to abolish them but to fulfil them. For truly, I say to you, till heaven and earth pass away, not an iota, not a dot, will pass from the law until all is accomplished. Whoever then relaxes one of the least of these commandments and teaches men so, shall be called least in the kingdom of heaven; but he who does them and teaches them shall be called great in the kingdom of heaven. For I tell you, unless your righteousness exceeds that of the scribes and Pharisees, you will never enter the kingdom of heaven. You have heard that it was said to the men of old, 'You shall not kill; and whoever kills shall be liable to judgment.' But I say to you that every one who is angry with his brother shall be liable to judgment; whoever insults his brother shall be liable to the council, and whoever says, 'You fool!' shall be liable to the hell of fire. So if you are offering your gift at the alter, and there remember that your brother has something against you, leave your gift there before the alter and go; first be reconciled to your brother, and then come and offer your gift." (*Matthew 5:17–24*)

Key Ideas: Christ completes the law
More than the letter of the law
Beyond anger to reconciliation

Action Step: Take the initiative to get acquainted with, listen to, and begin dialogue with persons of other races or social and economic classes or with groups antagonistic to your group in order to stimulate understanding.

Prayer: If I can dare to be a reconciler today, Lord, give me wisdom in the way to go about it.

26 THE BETTER WAY

"You have heard that it was said, 'An eye for an eye and a tooth for a tooth.' But I say to you, Do not resist one who is evil. But if any one strikes you on the right cheek, turn to him the other also; and if any one would sue you and take your coat, let him have your cloak as well; and if any one forces you to go one mile, go with him two miles. Give to him who begs from you, and do not refuse him who would borrow from you." (*Matthew 5:38–42*)

Key Ideas: The courage of nonretaliation
Values in addition to property
The challenge of the second mile

Action Step: Read a good biography telling of the spirit and style of life of one of the great prophets of nonviolent action and resistance.

Prayer: Today, Lord, I am determined to work out any anger I have peacefully, not by taking it out on uninvolved persons, especially my family.

27 THE GOLDEN RULE

"And as you wish that men would do to you, do so to them. If you love those who love you, what credit is that to you? For even sinners love those who love them. And if you do good to those who do good to you, what credit is that to you? For even sinners do the same. And if you lend to those from whom you hope to receive, what credit is that to you? Even sinners lend to sinners, to receive as much again. But love your enemies, and do good, and lend, expecting nothing in return; and your reward will be great, and you will be sons of the Most High; for he is kind to the ungrateful and the selfish. Be merciful, even as your Father is merciful." (*Luke 6:31–36*)

Key Ideas: Positive goodness
Loving the unlikeable
Loving our enemies

Action Step: Try to imagine how persons with whom you differ—other races, nationalities, school opponents, business competitors, rivals at work—think and feel; try putting yourself in their position.

Prayer: Lord, I will walk the road of love today by Your power and not turn back or aside to lesser ways.

28 QUIET GENEROSITY

"Thus, when you give alms, sound no trumpet before you, as the hypocrites do in the synagogues and in the streets, that they may be praised by men. Truly, I say to you, they have received their reward. But when you give alms, do not let your left hand know what your right hand is doing, so that your alms may be in secret; and your Father who sees in secret will reward you." (*Matthew 6:2–4*)

Key Ideas: Goodness for glory
Sharing with humility
Sometimes only God knows

Action Step: Put unpublicized generosity and charity to the test; see how God blesses such giving.

Prayer: Lord, I ask for a compassionate heart and common sense today in order to be able to help people who really need it.

29 THE UNIVERSAL PRAYER

"Pray then like this:

Our Father who art in heaven,
Hallowed by thy name.
Thy kingdom come,
Thy will be done,
On earth as it is in heaven.
Give us this day our daily bread;
And forgive us our debts,
As we also have forgiven our debtors;
And lead us not into temptation,
But deliver us from evil.

For if you forgive men their trespasses, your heavenly Father also will forgive you; but if you do not forgive men their trespasses, neither will your Father forgive your trespasses." (*Matthew 6:9–15*)

Key Ideas: Doing the Father's will
Receiving the Father's food
Sharing the Father's forgiveness

Action Step: Study and compare several New Testament translations of this foundational prayer of the Church.

Prayer: Lord, I feel full and free today having received from Your Son Jesus this central clue to continual communion with You.

30 TREASURES IN HEAVEN

"Do not lay up for yourselves treasures on earth, where moth and rust consume and where thieves break in and steal, but lay up for yourselves treasures in heaven, where neither moth nor rust consumes and where thieves do not break in and steal. For where your treasure is, there will your heart be also. The eye is the lamp of the body. So, if your eye is sound, your whole body will be full of light; but if your eye is not sound, your whole body will be full of darkness. If then the light in you is darkness, how great is the darkness! No one can serve two masters; for either he will hate the one and love the other, or he will be devoted to the one and despise the other. You cannot serve God and mammon." (*Matthew 6:19–24*)

Key Ideas: The Kingdom investment principle
Singular spiritual vision
Sometimes it is "either . . . or"

Action Step: For your local Christian fellowship or for your parish board, write down your vision of the Christian responsibility of stewardship of material and financial resources.

Prayer: Lead me today, Lord, into a sensible stewardship of spending, sharing, and saving of my money and financial resources.

31 A LIFE OF TRUST

"Therefore I tell you, do not be anxious about your life, what you shall eat or what you shall drink, nor about your body, what you shall put on. Is not life more than food, and the body more than clothing? Look at the birds of the air: they neither sow nor reap nor gather into barns, and yet your heavenly Father feeds them. Are you not of more value than they? And which of you by being anxious can add one cubit to his span of life? And why be anxious about clothing? Consider the lilies of the field, how they grow; they neither toil nor spin; yet I tell you, even Solomon in all his glory was not arrayed like one of these. But if God so clothes the grass of the field, which today is alive and tomorrow is thrown into the oven, will he not much more clothe you, O men of little faith? Therefore do not be anxious, saying, 'What shall we eat?' or 'What shall we drink?' or 'What shall we wear?' For the Gentiles seek all these things; and your heavenly Father knows that you need them all. But seek first his kingdom and his righteousness, and all these things shall be yours as well. Therefore do not be anxious about tomorrow, for tomorrow will be anxious for itself. Let the day's own trouble be sufficient for the day." (*Matthew 6:25–34*)

Key Ideas: Our persistent anxieties
Our heavenly Father's constant care
Our risk of total trust in God

Action Step: Rise early and spend some time out of doors—in your back yard, at a park, in the fields—observing and listening to the birds and animals.

Prayer: Today, Lord, it is wonderful that You see the sparrow and that You see even more in me.

32 HOW TO JUDGE

"Judge not, that you be not judged. For with the judgment you pronounce you will be judged, and the measure you give will be the measure you get. Why do you see the speck that is in your brother's eye, but do not notice the log that is in your own eye? Or how can you say to your brother, 'Let me take the speck out of your eye,' when there is the log in your own eye? You hypocrite, first take the log out of your own eye, and then you will see clearly to take the speck out of your brother's eye." (*Matthew 7:1–5*)

Key Ideas: Generosity in judgments
Distorted criticism
Clearing our vision

Action Step: Give a second look at the pressures being faced by persons you have been most critical of recently.

Prayer: Lord, I want to be more careful and kind today in my attitude toward others.

33 TREES AND FRUIT

"For no good tree bears bad fruit, nor again does a bad tree bear good fruit; for each tree is known by its own fruit. For figs are not gathered from thorns, nor are grapes picked from a bramble bush. The good man out of the good treasure of his heart produces good, and the evil man out of his evil treasure produces evil; for out of the abundance of the heart his mouth speaks." (*Luke 6:43–45*)

Key Ideas: Lesson from a fig tree
A choice of values
Character has its consequences

Action Step: Explore ways you may encourage the teaching of basic Christian values in the schools—balanced curricula, quality teaching, adequate resources, and so forth.

Prayer: Lord, keep me moving today beyond the mere surface decoration of myself toward a deeper development of my personality and character.

34 BUILDING OUR LIVES

"Every one then who hears these words of mine and does them will be like a wise man who built his house upon the rock; and the rain fell, and the flood came, and the winds blew and beat upon that house, but it did not fall, because it had been founded on the rock. And every one who hears these words of mine and does not do them will be like a foolish man who built his house upon the sand; and the rain fell, and the floods came, and the winds blew and beat against that house, and it fell; and great was the fall of it." (*Matthew 7:24–27*)

Key Ideas: Everyone is building
Some build wisely
Others build blindly

Action Step: Listen carefully to the sermon next Sunday, and follow through Monday through Saturday on the Word of God you have heard.

Prayer: Thank You, Lord, for showing me the way today of doing Your will, so that I may have something solid to stand upon.

35 THE MESSIAH'S MINISTRY

And John, calling to him two of his disciples, sent them to the Lord, saying, "Are you he who is to come, or shall we look for another?" And when the men had come to him, they said, "John the Baptist has sent us to you, saying, 'Are you he who is to come, or shall we look for another?' " In that hour he cured many of diseases and plagues and evil spirits, and on many that were blind he bestowed sight. And he answered them, "Go and tell John what you have seen and heard: the blind receive their sight, the lame walk, lepers are cleansed, and the deaf hear, the dead are raised up, the poor have good news preached to them. And blessed is he who takes no offense at me." (*Luke 7:19–23*)

Key Ideas: Inquiring about the Messiah
Help for the hopeless
The signs of the servant ministry

Action Step: Become a supporter of one of your church's frontier missions of compassion to our suffering world.

Prayer: Lord, I hope people will conclude by my actions and concern for others today that I am a follower of Jesus the Christ.

36 YOKEFELLOWS WITH CHRIST

"Come to me, all who labor and are heavy laden, and I will give you rest. Take my yoke upon you, and learn from me; for I am gentle and lowly in heart, and you will find rest for your souls. For my yoke is easy, and my burden is light." (*Matthew 11:28–30*)

Key Ideas: A universal invitation of Christ
Christ Himself is our yoke
Relief in a strange way

Action Step: Plan a workshop at your church on the subject "A Christian Prescription for Anxiety"; invite a doctor, psychologist, a member of the clergy, and a member of the laity to lead.

Prayer: If I should back away from Your demands today, Lord, I know I shall shortcircuit the possibility of finding lasting peace within my inmost self.

37 EQUAL PARTNERS

Soon afterward he went on through cities and villages, preaching and bringing the good news of the kingdom of God. And the twelve were with him, and also some women who had been healed of evil spirits and infirmities: Mary, called Magdalene, from whom seven demons had gone out, and Joanna, the wife of Chuza, Herod's steward, and Susanna, and many others, who provided for them out of their means. (*Luke 8:1–3*)

Key Ideas: Jesus, the Evangelist
Dedicated women disciples
Material stewardship for ministry

Action Step: Evaluate the participation of women as well as men in the leadership of your Christian fellowship.

Prayer: Lord, with Your inspiration today, I will treat my fellow workers as persons in their own right, whether they be male or female.

38 THE DISASTER OF DIVISION

Knowing their thoughts, he said to them, "Every kingdom divided against itself is laid waste, and no city or house divided against itself will stand; and if Satan casts out Satan, he is divided against himself; how then will his kingdom stand? And if I cast out demons by Beelzebul, by whom do your sons cast them out? Therefore they shall be your judges. But if it is by the Spirit of God that I cast out demons, then the kingdom of God has come upon you." (*Matthew 12:25–28*)

Key Ideas: Spiritual civil war
Encountering evil
Deliverance from demons

Action Step: Make a pyramid chart of your most significant loyalties and life motivations; can you place the God of the universe at the top of your pyramid of personal values and as the integrative Force of your life?

Prayer: Today, Lord, destroy every divisive force within my inmost self in order that I might be one strong, singular self.

39 PROPHETS OF REPENTANCE

Then some of the scribes and Pharisees said to him, "Teacher, we wish to see a sign from you." But he answered them, "An evil and adulterous generation seeks a sign; but no sign shall be given to it except the sign of the prophet Jonah. For as Jonah was three days and three nights in the belly of the whale, so will the Son of man be three days and three nights in the heart of the earth. The men of Nineveh will arise at the judgment with this generation and condemn it; for they repented at the preaching of Jonah, and behold, something greater than Jonah is here." (*Matthew 12:38–41*)

Key Ideas: Overlooking God's previous grace
Jonah and Jesus
The test of hearing God's Word

Action Step: Listen carefully to what some of the contemporary prophets—national leaders, scientists, judges, authors, preachers—are saying to our world.

Prayer: Lord, I'm going to live today in the reality of Jesus' resurrection.

40 OVERCOMING EVIL

"When the unclean spirit has gone out of a man, he passes through waterless places seeking rest, but he finds none. Then he says, 'I will return to my house from which I came.' And when he comes he finds it empty, swept, and put in order. Then he goes and brings with him seven other spirits more evil than himself, and they enter and dwell there; and the last state of that man becomes worse than the first. So shall it be also with this evil generation." (*Matthew 12:43–45*)

Key Ideas: Expelling evil is not easy
Evil's opportunity in a vacuum
The end of an evil age

Action Step: Invite a friend who is trying to break out of an old destructive pattern of life to go with you or start out on some new growth, service, or recreational experience with you.

Prayer: Keep me on guard today, Lord, lest I settle for a bland, uncommitted goodness that cannot withstand the vicious forces of evil that may seek my allegiance.

41 JESUS' FAMILY

And his mother and his brothers came; and standing outside they sent to him and called him. And a crowd was sitting about him; and they said to him, "Your mother and your brothers are outside, asking for you." And he answered, "Who are my mother and my brothers?" And looking around on those who sat about him, he said, "Here are my mother and my brothers! Whoever does the will of God is my brother, and sister, and mother." (*Mark 3:31–35*)

Key Ideas: Jesus' blood relatives
A probing question
A key to new community

Action Step: Speak to a lonely and frustrated person of the riches of friendship, support, and challenge in vital and continual involvement in the Church.

Prayer: I thank You today, Lord, for giving to me a whole new and larger family because of Jesus, Your Christ.

42 SOILS AND SOULS

And he taught them many things in parables, and in his teaching he said to them: "Listen! A sower went out to sow. And as he sowed, some seed fell along the path, and the birds came and devoured it. Other seed fell on rocky ground, where it had not much soil, and immediately it sprang up, since it had no depth of soil; and when the sun rose it was scorched, and since it had no root it withered away. Other seed fell among thorns and the thorns grew up and choked it, and it yielded no grain. And other seeds fell into good soil and brought forth grain, growing up and increasing and yielding thirtyfold and sixtyfold and a hundredfold." And he said, "He who has ears to hear, let him hear." (*Mark 4:2–9*)

Key Ideas: Faith to sow the seed
Unproductive soils
Harvest from the good soil

Action Step: Make a systematic inquiry into the reasons why people have dropped out of your church life or turned away from active support of the cause of Christ to which you are related.

Prayer: Lord, I intend to scatter Your Good News today and not be discouraged if some people do not respond.

43 A TIME FOR WAITING

And he said, "The kingdom of God is as if a man should scatter seed upon the ground, and should sleep and rise night and day, and the seed should sprout and grow, he knows not how. The earth produces of itself, first the blade, then the ear, then the full grain in the ear. But when the grain is ripe, at once he puts in the sickle, because the harvest has come." *(Mark 4:26–29)*

Key Ideas: Planting within our power
Patient trust in power
Power within and around us

Action Step: In the midst of much planning and work on a project, step back for a moment and ask, How am I participating in the activity of God already present in this task?

Prayer: Lord, I will not be anxious today over that which is only within Your power to accomplish.

44 FINDING THE KINGDOM

"The kingdom of heaven is like treasure hidden in a field, which a man found and covered up; then in his joy he goes and sells all that he has and buys that field. Again, the kingdom of heaven is like a merchant in search of fine pearls, who, on finding one pearl of great value, went and sold all that he had and bought it. Again, the kingdom of heaven is like a net which was thrown into the sea and gathered fish of every kind; when it was full, men drew it ashore and sat down and sorted the good into vessels but threw away the bad. So it will be at the close of the age. The angels will come out and separate the evil from the righteous, and throw them into the furnace of fire; there men will weep and gnash their teeth. Have you understood all this?" They said to him, "Yes." And he said to them, "Therefore every scribe who has been trained for the kingdom of heaven is like a householder who brings out of his treasure what is new and what is old." *(Matthew 13:44–52)*

Key Ideas: The treasures of God's Kingdom

The discoveries of God's Kingdom
The joys of God's Kingdom

Action Step: There surely is for you some unexplored sector or segment of our life and world; start a plan for investigating that field of human experience with a view to seeing it from a Christian perspective.

Prayer: Lord, I want to keep searching today and always for new secrets of Your Kingdom life that I believe You have placed in this world as delightful gifts along the way.

45 CHRIST IN OUR BOAT

One day he got into a boat with his disciples, and he said to them, "Let us go across to the other side of the lake." So they set out, and as they sailed he fell asleep. And a storm of wind came down on the lake, and they were filling with water, and were in danger. And they went and woke him, saying, "Master, Master, we are perishing!" And he awoke and rebuked the wind and the raging waves; and they ceased, and there was a calm. He said to them, "Where is your faith?" And they were afraid, and they marveled, saying to one another, "Who then is this, that he commands even wind and water, and they obey him?" (*Luke 8:22–25*)

Key Ideas: The threatening storms
A question of faith
The Master's composure

Action Step: Anticipate an emergency situation and alternative for facing it without being paralyzed by panic.

Prayer: I am strengthened, Lord, when I know You are in the boat of life with me today.

46 A HEALTHY MIND

The herdsmen fled, and told it in the city and in the country. And people came to see what it was that had happened. And they came to Jesus, and saw the demoniac sitting there, clothed and in his right mind, the man who had had the legion; and they were afraid. And those who had seen it told what had happened to the demoniac and to the swine. And they began to beg Jesus to depart from their neighborhood. And as he was getting into the boat, the man who had been possessed with demons begged him that he might be with him. But he refused, and said to him, "Go home to your friends, and tell them how much the Lord has done for you, and how he has had mercy on you." And he went away and began to proclaim in the Decapolis how much Jesus had done for him; and all men marveled. (*Mark 5:14–20*)

Key Ideas: Indisputable evidence
"Jesus, go home!"
What follows conversion?

Action Step: Discover and evaluate the mental health counseling and therapy services with which your church can cooperate in your community.

Prayer: I am filled with deep rejoicing today, Lord, to be able to live through one day of good mental health.

47 JESUS' UNIQUE AUTHORITY

And coming to his own country he taught them in their synagogue, so that they were astonished, and said, "Where did this man get this wisdom and these mighty works? Is not this the carpenter's son? Is not his mother called Mary? And are not his brothers James and Joseph and Simon and Judas? And are not all his sisters with us? Where then did this man get all this?" And they took offense at him. But Jesus said to them, "A prophet is not without honor except in his own country and in his own house." And he did not do many mighty works there, because of their unbelief. (*Matthew 13:54–58*)

Key Ideas: Surprising the home town
Jesus' blood relatives
The frustration of resistance

Action Step: Be fair with persons you have known for years, looking for ways they may have grown in personality and abilities.

Prayer: Lord, if people misjudge my abilities today I will work with those who are ready to respond.

48 MANY IN NEED

And Jesus went about all the cities and villages, teaching in their synagogues and preaching the gospel of the kingdom, and healing every disease and every infirmity. When he saw the crowds, he had compassion for them, because they were harassed and helpless, like sheep without a shepherd. Then he said to his disciples, "The harvest is plentiful, but the laborers are few; pray therefore the Lord of the harvest to send out laborers into his harvest." (*Matthew 9:35–38*)

Key Ideas: Jesus' comprehensive ministry
Jesus' caring for the masses
Jesus' call for workers

Action Step: Consider how to expand to a larger mission the effective work of your local church.

Prayer: Lord, without Your inspiration today I will not be able to enlist others into the Christian mission and ministry.

49 FACING THREATS

"Lo, I send you out as sheep in the midst of wolves; so be wise as serpents and innocent as doves. Beware of men; for they will deliver you up to councils, and flog you in their synagogues, and you will be dragged before governors and kings for my sake, to bear testimony before them and the Gentiles. When they deliver you up, do not be anxious how you are to speak or what you are to say; for what you are to say will be given to you in that hour; for it is not you who speak, but the Spirit of your Father speaking through you." (*Matthew 10:16–20*)

Key Ideas: Strategy in conflicts
Courage before authorities
Creativity through crises

Action Step: When you are inclined to overreact, carefully think things through first.

Prayer: Empower me, Lord, to be faithful to You and fearless in my conversations today.

"And do not fear those who kill the body but cannot kill the soul; rather fear him who can destroy both soul and body in hell. Are not two sparrows sold for a penny? And not one of them will fall to the ground without your Father's will. But even the hairs of your head are all numbered. Fear not, therefore; you are of more value than many sparrows. So every one who acknowledges me before men, I also will acknowledge before my Father who is in heaven; but whoever denies me before men, I also will deny before my Father who is in heaven." (*Matthew 10:28–33*)

Key Ideas: The fear that matters
Our Father watches over us
Our confession of faith reaches heaven

Action Step: Go back into that difficult and threatening situation—at work, school, church, union, club, or home—stand true to your ideals and faith, regardless of the consequences.

Prayer: Today, Lord, I am convinced that I cannot endure without Your help that which Christians are suffering in our world and which I too may be called upon to suffer.

51 CUP OF COLD WATER

"He who receives you receives me, and he who receives me receives him who sent me. He who receives a prophet because he is a prophet shall receive a prophet's reward, and he who receives a righteous man because he is a righteous man shall receive a righteous man's reward. And whoever gives to one of these little ones even a cup of cold water because he is a disciple, truly, I say to you, he shall not lose his reward." (*Matthew 10:40–42*)

Key Ideas: The divine-human fellowship
The blessings of generosity
The fellowship of the shared cup

Action Step: Have a good conversation with your pastor or a pastor friend; ask what is a major concern he or she may have with regard to his or her church.

Prayer: Seemingly small things will be significant today for me, Lord, because I know it is in such happenings that I may find You most real.

"Do not labor for the food which perishes, but for the food which endures to eternal life, which the Son of man will give to you; for on him has God the Father set his seal." Then they said to him, "What must we do, to be doing the work of God?" Jesus answered them, "This is the work of God, that you believe in him whom he has sent." So they said to him, "Then what sign do you do, that we may see, and believe you? What work do you perform? Our fathers ate the manna in the wilderness; as it is written, 'He gave them bread from heaven to eat.' " Jesus then said to them, "Truly, truly, I say to you, it was not Moses who gave you the bread from heaven; my Father gives you the true bread from heaven. For the bread of God is that which comes down from heaven, and gives life to the world." They said to him, "Lord, give us this bread always." Jesus said to them, "I am the bread of life; he who comes to me shall not hunger, and he who believes in me shall never thirst. But I said to you that you have seen me and yet do not believe. All that the Father gives me will come to me; and him who comes to me I will not cast out. For I have come down from heaven, not to do my own will, but the will of him who sent me; and this is the will of him who sent me, that I should lose nothing of all that he has given me, but raise it up at the last day. For this is the will of my Father, that every one who sees the Son and believes in him should have eternal life; and I will raise him up at the last day." *(John 6:27–40)*

Key Ideas: Bread for the soul
Bread from heaven
Bread for eternal life

Action Step: List your activities, projects, and meetings next week; spend some time considering these concerns, noting which ones are really significant and which are a careless use of your talents and energies.

Prayer: Thanks and praise be to You, Lord, for today I am fed by nourishing spiritual food that brings me enduring satisfactions.

53 PURITY FROM WITHIN

And he called the people to him and said to them, "Hear and understand: not what goes into the mouth defiles a man, but what comes out of the mouth, this defiles a man." Then the disciples came and said to him, "Do you know that the Pharisees were offended when they heard this saying?" He answered, "Every plant which my heavenly Father has not planted will be rooted up. Let them alone; they are blind guides. And if a blind man leads a blind man, both will fall into a pit." But Peter said to him, "Explain the parable to us." And he said, "Are you also still without understanding? Do you not see that whatever goes into the mouth passes into the stomach, and so passes on? But what comes out of the mouth proceeds from the heart, and this defiles a man. For out of the heart come evil thoughts, murder, adultery, fornication, theft, false witness, slander. These are what defile a man; but to eat with unwashed hands does not defile a man." (*Matthew 15:10–20*)

Key Ideas: Food laws are not enough
Critics will be judged too
The true test of holiness

Action Step: Think of your major criticism of the churches, and then show someone a way Christians are trying to correct that error.

Prayer: Lord, I will live by the most important rules today, the ones that prevent me from feeling spiritually superior to others.

54 DUTY TO PARENTS

And he said to them, "You have a fine way of rejecting the commandment of God, in order to keep your tradition! For Moses said, 'Honor your father and your mother'; and, 'He who speaks evil of father or mother, let him surely die'; but you say, 'If a man tells his father or his mother, What you would have gained from me is Corban' (that is, given to God)—then you no longer permit him to do anything for his father or mother, thus making void the word of God through your tradition which you hand on." (*Mark 7:9–13*)

Key Ideas: Religious "irresponsibility"
Interpreting away the truth
Rejecting the Word through tradition

Action Step: Do something with your parents, with the parents of friends, or with neighbors that will help them to find greater joy in living.

Prayer: Today, Lord, I cannot hide behind Your clear commandments by means of any technical logic or rational argument.

55 FRIEND OF THE BLIND

And they came to Bethsaida. And some people brought to him a blind man, and begged him to touch him. And he took the blind man by the hand, and led him out of the village; and when he had spit on his eyes and laid his hands upon him, he asked him, "Do you see anything?" And he looked up and said, "I see men; but they look like trees, walking." Then again he laid his hands upon his eyes; and he looked intently and was restored, and saw everything clearly. And he sent him away to his home, saying, "Do not even enter the village." (*Mark 8:22–26*)

Key Ideas: Hoping for a miracle
The Master's touch
The blessing of sight

Action Step: Bring someone within the sphere of Christ's healing powers; acquaint them with your life of prayer and trust in God.

Prayer: Lord, today I want to be a friend of the blind in body, mind, and soul.

56 GOD'S PERSONAL REVELATION

Now when Jesus came into the district of Caesarea Philippi, he asked his disciples, "Who do men say that the Son of man is?" And they said, "Some say John the Baptist, others say Elijah, and others Jeremiah or one of the prophets." He said to them, "But who do you say that I am?" Simon Peter replied, "You are the Christ, the Son of the living God." And Jesus answered him, "Blessed are you, Simon Bar-Jona! For flesh and blood has not revealed this to you, but my Father who is in heaven. And I tell you, you are Peter, and on this rock I will build my church, and the powers of death shall not prevail against it. I will give you the keys of the kingdom of heaven, and whatever you bind on earth shall be bound in heaven, and whatever you loose on earth shall be loosed in heaven." (*Matthew 16:13–19*)

Key Ideas: In the company of the prophets
The central creed of Christianity
The prevailing power of the Church

Action Step: Encourage freedom within your Christian fellowship so that individuals may freely tell of their personal allegiance to Jesus the Christ.

Prayer: Lord, I will use no other test of fellowship for my associations with other Christians than our common allegiance to Jesus Christ.

57 A DAILY CROSS

And he said to all, "If any man would come after me, let him deny himself and take up his cross daily and follow me. For whoever would save his life will lose it; and whoever loses his life for my sake, he will save it. For what does it profit a man if he gains the whole world and loses or forfeits himself? For whoever is ashamed of me and of my words, of him will the Son of man be ashamed when he comes in his glory and the glory of the Father and of the holy angels." (*Luke 9:23–26*)

Key Ideas: The denial of selfishness
The discovery of our true self
The dedication of self to a Savior

Action Step: Do something by writing, conversation, behavior, or being present that publicly identifies you as a follower of Jesus Your Christ.

Prayer: Lead me today, Lord, from worry over myself into a life of concern and caring for others.

58 MOUNTAIN VISIONS

And after six days Jesus took with him Peter and James and John, and led them up a high mountain apart by themselves; and he was transfigured before them, and his garments became glistening, intensely white, as no fuller on earth could bleach them. And there appeared to them Elijah with Moses; and they were talking to Jesus. And Peter said to Jesus, "Master, it is well that we are here; let us make three booths, one for you and one for Moses and one for Elijah." For he did not know what to say, for they were exceedingly afraid. And a cloud overshadowed them, and a voice came out of the cloud, "This is my beloved Son; listen to him." And suddenly looking around they no longer saw any one with them but Jesus only. (*Mark 9:2–8*)

Key Ideas: Christ's glistening presence
Peter's fumbling recognition
God's clarifying Word

Action Step: Turn to a good Bible commentary, and see how much Jesus had in common with His spiritual forefathers—Moses and Elijah.

Prayer: Lord, I cherish the visions of the mountain heights today as a resource of Your Spirit when my mood is all plains and valleys.

59 MUSTARD SEED FAITH

And when they came to the crowd, a man came up to him and kneeling before him said, "Lord, have mercy on my son, for he is an epileptic and he suffers terribly; for often he falls into the fire, and often into the water. And I brought him to your disciples, and they could not heal him." And Jesus answered, "O faithless perverse generation, how long am I to be with you? How long am I to bear with you? Bring him here to me." And Jesus rebuked him, and the demon came out of him, and the boy was cured instantly. Then the disciples came to Jesus privately and said, "Why could we not cast it out?" He said to them, "Because of your little faith. For truly, I say to you, if you have faith as a grain of mustard seed, you will say to this mountain, 'Move from here to there,' and it will move; and nothing will be impossible to you." (*Matthew 17:14–20*)

Key Ideas: The burden of helping others
The frustration of a teacher
The tremendous power of faith

Action Step: Undertake an assignment or project big enough to require a deep reliance upon God to accomplish it well.

Prayer: Today, Lord, I will seek to develop my spiritual skills to match other skills for service to those in need.

60 FAIRNESS TOWARD OTHERS

John said to him, "Teacher, we saw a man casting out demons in your name, and we forbade him, because he was not following us." But Jesus said, "Do not forbid him; for no one who does a mighty work in my name will be able soon after to speak evil of me. For he that is not against us is for us." (*Mark 9:38–40*)

Key Ideas: Credentials for doing good
The fellowship of healing
A principle for understanding

Action Step: Learn about the work of Christian benevolence and witnessing of another denomination and how many churches are involved in cooperative projects.

Prayer: Today I am determined to do good, Lord, regardless of who gets the credit.

61 SERIOUSNESS OF SIN

"And if your hand causes you to sin, cut it off; it is better for you to enter life maimed than with two hands to go to hell, to the unquenchable fire. And if your foot causes you to sin, cut it off; it is better for you to enter life lame than with two feet to be thrown into hell. And if your eye causes you to sin, pluck it out; it is better for you to enter the kingdom of God with one eye than with two eyes to be thrown into hell, where their worm does not die and the fire is not quenched." (*Mark 9:43–48*)

Key Ideas: Radical remedy for sin
Radical consequences of sin
Radical reward for discipline

Action Step: Examine your own bad habits, and try to correct them before you seek to change others.

Prayer: Today I dedicate my body to You, Lord, to be an instrument of Your will.

62 COVENANT COMMUNITY

"Truly, I say to you, whatever you bind on earth will be bound in heaven, and whatever you loose on earth will be loosed in heaven. Again I say to you, if two of you agree on earth about anything they ask, it will be done for them by my Father in heaven. For where two or three are gathered in my name, there am I in the midst of them." (*Matthew 18:18–20*)

Key Ideas: Together for ministry
Together in prayer
Together with Christ

Action Step: Formulate with other Christians the marks of a great church; find some ways to hold these ideals before your congregation or parish.

Prayer: Lord, I am going to work with others in my church today in the Spirit of Christ.

63 TEACHER FROM GOD

About the middle of the feast Jesus went up into the temple and taught. The Jews marveled at it, saying, "How is it that this man has learning, when he has never studied?" So Jesus answered them, "My teaching is not mine, but his who sent me; if any man's will is to do his will, he shall know whether the teaching is from God or whether I am speaking on my own authority. He who speaks on his own authority seeks his own glory; but he who seeks the glory of him who sent him is true, and in him there is no falsehood." *(John 7:14–18)*

Key Ideas: The remarkable wisdom of Jesus
The discovery of truth by doing
The authority of Jesus' humility

Action Step: Try practicing the experimental logic that Jesus taught; test out Jesus' teaching on unselfish assistance to others.

Prayer: Lord, if I can apply the best scientific principles to my spiritual growth today, I will do so.

64 STONES OF CONDEMNATION

Early in the morning he came again to the temple; all the people came to him, and he sat down and taught them. The scribes and the Pharisees brought a woman who had been caught in adultery, and placing her in the midst they said to him, "Teacher, this woman has been caught in the act of adultery. Now in the law Moses commanded us to stone such. What do you say about her?" This they said to test him, that they might have some charge to bring against him. Jesus bent down and wrote with his finger on the ground. And as they continued to ask him, he stood up and said to them, "Let him who is without sin among you be the first to throw a stone at her." And once more he bent down and wrote with his finger on the ground. But when they heard it, they went away, one by one, beginning with the eldest, and Jesus was left alone with the woman standing before him. Jesus looked up and said to her, "Woman, where are they? Has no one condemned you?" She said, "No one, Lord." And Jesus said, "Neither do I condemn you; go, and do not sin again." *(John 8:2–11)*

Key Ideas: A woman trapped in sin
The sinless may condemn
New hope with Christ her Friend

Action Step: Remember how you may have been treated in a time of trouble; determine then to meet each person with respect to their individual backgrounds, needs, and willingness to try rather than as a stereotyped "problem," "case," or "condition."

Prayer: Lord, I will face up to my sins today since in Your mercy there is the possibility of beginning again.

65 TRUTH THAT FREES

Jesus then said to the Jews who had believed in him, "If you continue in my word, you are truly my disciples, and you will know the truth, and the truth will make you free." They answered him, "We are descendents of Abraham, and have never been in bondage to anyone. How is it that you say, 'You will be made free'?" Jesus answered them, "Truly, truly, I say to you, every one who commits sin is a slave to sin. The slave does not continue in the house forever; the son continues forever. So if the Son makes you free, you will be free indeed." (*John 8:31–36*)

Key Ideas: The journey toward the truth
Limitations of inheritance
The freedom of children of God

Action Step: Do some thinking about the nature of the truth Jesus offers us that makes it a liberating force in our lives.

Prayer: Since You have made me free, Lord, help me today to stay as free as love and responsibility will allow.

66 THE GOOD SHEPHERD

So Jesus again said to them, "Truly, truly, I say to you, I am the door of the sheep. All who came before me are thieves and robbers; but the sheep did not heed them. I am the door; if any one enters by me, he will be saved, and will go in and out and find pasture. The thief comes only to steal and kill and destroy; I came that they may have life, and have it abundantly. I am the good shepherd. The good shepherd lays down his life for the sheep. He who is a hireling and not a shepherd, whose own the sheep are not, sees the wolf coming and leaves the sheep and flees; and the wolf snatches them and scatters them. He flees because he is a hireling and cares nothing for the sheep. I am the good shepherd; I know my own and my own know me, as the Father knows me and I know the Father; and I lay down my life for the sheep. And I have other sheep, that are not of this fold; I must bring them also, and they will heed my voice. So there shall be one flock, one shepherd." (*John 10:7–16*)

Key Ideas: The Shepherd of abundant life
The test of a true shepherd
The larger flock of God

Action Step: List in your prayer of thanksgiving at the dinner table those qualities which for you make life overflowing and meaningful.

Prayer: Lord, if I am able to live and work in harmony with other Christians today, it surely will be because of Your directing love.

67 TWO BY TWO

After this the Lord appointed seventy others, and sent them on ahead of him, two by two, into every town and place where he himself was about to come. And he said to them, "The harvest is plentiful, but the laborers are few; pray therefore the Lord of the harvest to send out laborers into his harvest. Go your way; behold, I send you out as lambs in the midst of wolves. Carry no purse, no bag, no sandals; and salute no one on the road. Whatever house you enter, first say, 'Peace be to this house!' And if a son of peace is there, your peace shall rest upon him; but if not, it shall return to you. And remain in the same house, eating and drinking what they provide, for the laborer deserves his wages; do not go from house to house. Whenever you enter a town and they receive you, eat what is set before you; heal the sick in it and say to them, 'The kingdom of God has come near to you.' But whenever you enter a town and they do not receive you, go into its streets and say, 'Even the dust of your town that clings to our feet, we wipe off against you; nevertheless know this, that the kingdom of God has come near.' " (*Luke 10:1–11*)

Key Ideas: Mutual support witnessing
Carry the peace of God with you
Don't let rejection get you down

Action Step: Make a strategic visit with your husband, wife, or good friend to a person or family that has no church connection; welcome them to your church worship or to the activities of one of its groups.

Prayer: Lord, I want to use my best skills in communication today in showing Christian friendship to others.

68 EVIL ENCOUNTERED

The seventy returned with joy, saying, "Lord, even the demons are subject to us in your name!" And he said to them, "I saw Satan fall like lightning from heaven. Behold, I have given you authority to tread upon serpents and scorpions, and over all the power of the enemy; and nothing shall hurt you. Nevertheless do not rejoice in this, that the spirits are subject to you; but rejoice that your names are written in heaven." *(Luke 10:17–20)*

Key Ideas: Sharing joy
A vision of victory
Right rejoicing

Action Step: Recall some of your personal abilities that you now almost take for granted; trace them back to the persons or experiences that helped you acquire them.

Prayer: Lord, if I am able to experience spiritual successes today, keep my head clear concerning who deserves the credit.

69 THE GOOD SAMARITAN

But he, desiring to justify himself, said to Jesus, "And who is my neighbor?" Jesus replied, "A man was going down from Jerusalem to Jericho, and he fell among robbers, who stripped him and beat him, and departed, leaving him half dead. Now by chance a priest was going down that road; and when he saw him he passed by on the other side. So likewise a Levite, when he came to the place and saw him, passed by on the other side. But a Samaritan, as he journeyed, came to where he was; and when he saw him, he had compassion, and went to him and bound up his wounds, pouring on oil and wine; then he set him on his own beast and brought him to an inn, and took care of him. And the next day he took out two denarii and gave them to the innkeeper, saying, 'Take care of him; and whatever more you spend, I will repay you when I come back.' Which of these three, do you think, proved neighbor to the man who fell among the robbers?" He said, "The one who showed mercy on him." And Jesus said to him, "Go and do likewise." (*Luke 10:29–37*)

Key Ideas: A dangerous question
Getting involved in human need
We finish the story

Action Step: Present a description to your congregation's Sunday school class, social action committee, or official church board of the various ways people are hurting right in your own community.

Prayer: Lord, move me today to get off of my comfortable position and reach out to help persons in need find a way of recovery.

70 TWO WAYS TO SERVE

Now as they went on their way, he entered a village; and a woman named Martha received him into her house. And she had a sister called Mary, who sat at the Lord's feet and listened to his teaching. But Martha was distracted with much serving; and she went to him and said, "Lord, do you not care that my sister has left me to serve alone? Tell her then to help me." But the Lord answered her, "Martha, Martha, you are anxious and troubled about many things; one thing is needful. Mary has chosen the good portion, which shall not be taken away from her." (*Luke 10:38–42*)

Key Ideas: Taking time to learn
Anxious hospitality
The calming word

Action Step: Work out a plan in your family for sharing household chores so that every member has regular opportunities to relax and do something for personal enrichment.

Prayer: Today, Lord, forgive me my daily frets.

71 ASK, SEEK, KNOCK

And he said to them, "Which of you who has a friend will go to him at midnight and say to him, 'Friend, lend me three loaves; for a friend of mine has arrived on a journey, and I have nothing to set before him'; and he will answer from within, 'Do not bother me; the door is now shut, and my children are with me in bed; I cannot get up and give you anything'? I tell you, though he will not get up and give him anything because he is his friend, yet because of his importunity he will rise and give him whatever he needs. And I tell you, Ask, and it will be given you; seek, and you will find; knock, and it will be opened to you. For every one who asks receives, and he who seeks finds, and to him who knocks it will be opened. What father among you, if his son asks for a fish, will instead of a fish give him a serpent; or if he asks for an egg, will give him a scorpion? If you then, who are evil, know how to give good gifts to your children, how much more will the heavenly Father give the Holy Spirit to those who ask him?" (*Luke 11:5–13*)

Key Ideas: Human need
Active prayer
Creative love

Action Step: Follow up on your concern and awakened conscience with concerted compassion for human suffering.

Prayer: Use my hands and feet and voice today, Lord, as instruments of Your purposes for our world.

72 A PROGRAM FOR LIFE

And he said to them, "Take heed, and beware of all covetousness; for a man's life does not consist in the abundance of his possessions." And he told them a parable, saying, "The land of a rich man brought forth plentifully; and he thought to himself, 'What shall I do, for I have nowhere to store my crops?' And he said, 'I will do this: I will pull down my barns, and build larger ones; and there I will store all my grain and my goods. And I will say to my soul, Soul, you have ample goods laid up for many years; take your ease, eat, drink, be merry.' But God said to him, 'Fool! This night your soul is required of you; and the things you have prepared, whose will they be?' So is he who lays up treasure for himself, and is not rich toward God." (*Luke 12:15–21*)

Key Ideas: The choices of the prosperous
The false confidence of the careless
The consequences of spiritual poverty

Action Step: Discuss with some friends how a Christian can determine the difference between necessities and luxuries.

Prayer: Lord, puncture my feelings of false security today before I waste my years or lose my sense of values.

73 INACCURATE COMPARISONS

There were some present at that very time who told him of the Galileans whose blood Pilate had mingled with their sacrifices. And he answered them, "Do you think that these Galileans were worse sinners than all the other Galileans, because they suffered thus? I tell you, No; but unless you repent you will all likewise perish. Or those eighteen upon whom the tower in Siloam fell and killed them, do you think that they were worse offenders than all the others who dwelt in Jerusalem? I tell you, No; but unless you repent you will all likewise perish." (*Luke 13:1–5*)

Key Ideas: Evaluating human violence
Assessing natural calamity
No exemption from repentance

Action Step: Stop expecting everyone else to do the changing; give evidence by your own life that you are willing to be a part of the fellowship of repentance.

Prayer: While I must evaluate others today, Lord, I would work to correct my own sins as well.

74 POWER TO TRANSFORM

He said therefore, "What is the kingdom of God like? And to what shall I compare it? It is like a grain of mustard seed which a man took and sowed in his garden; and it grew and became a tree, and the birds of the air made nests in its branches." And again he said, "To what shall I compare the kingdom of God? It is like leaven which a woman took and hid in three measures of flour, till it was all leavened." (*Luke 13:18–21*)

Key Ideas: The spiritual in the earthly
How the Kingdom grows
How the Kingdom expands

Action Step: Plant some seedling thoughts and inspirations about love and justice in your circles of influence.

Prayer: Lord, give me a faith today to see the worthwhileness of small but significant efforts for good.

75 THE KINGDOM OPPORTUNITY

"Strive to enter by the narrow door; for many, I tell you, will seek to enter and will not be able. When once the householder has risen up and shut the door, you will begin to stand outside and to knock at the door, saying, 'Lord, open to us.' He will answer you, 'I do not know where you come from.' Then you will begin to say, 'We ate and drank in your presence, and you taught in our streets.' But he will say, 'I tell you, I do not know where you come from; depart from me, all you workers of iniquity!' There you will weep and gnash your teeth, when you see Abraham and Isaac and Jacob and all the prophets in the kingdom of God and you yourselves thrust out. And men will come from east and west, and from north and south, and sit at table in the kingdom of God. And behold, some are last who will be first, and some are first who will be last." (*Luke 13:24–30*)

Key Ideas: The door to life is open
A special privilege has its limits
The guest list of the heavenly banquet

Action Step: Invite some persons from another culture or race to dinner—foreign students, a refugee family, fellow workers, or neighbors.

Prayer: Lord, today I am proud to be a part of a worldwide Christianity that draws into itself the riches of the cultural contributions of the nations into the service of Jesus Christ.

76 ONLY FOR THE HUNGRY

When one of those who sat at table with him heard this, he said to him, "Blessed is he who shall eat bread in the kingdom of God!" But he said to him, "A man once gave a great banquet, and invited many; and at the time for the banquet he sent his servant to say to those who had been invited, 'Come; for all is now ready.' But they all alike began to make excuses. The first said to him, 'I have bought a field, and I must go out and see it; I pray you, have me excused.' And another said, 'I have bought five yoke of oxen, and I go to examine them; I pray you, have me excused.' And another said, 'I have married a wife, and therefore I cannot come.' So the servant came and reported this to his master. Then the householder in anger said to his servant, 'Go out quickly to the streets and lanes of the city, and bring in the poor and maimed and blind and lame.' And the servant said, 'Sir, what you commanded has been done, and still there is room.' And the master said to the servant, 'Go out to the highways and hedges, and compel people to come in, that my house may be filled. For I tell you, none of those men who were invited shall taste my banquet.' " (*Luke 14:15–24*)

Key Ideas: Life is an invitation
We must choose
Our chance may pass

Action Step: Surprise someone with frank and sincere speech; simply avoid all evasive and rationalizing talk.

Prayer: Today, Lord, when invitations arise to engage in Your Kingdom opportunities, I will reply with a ready life.

77 A CROSS FOR EVERYONE

"Whoever does not bear his own cross and come after me, cannot be my disciple. For which of you, desiring to build a tower, does not first sit down and count the cost, whether he has enough to complete it? Otherwise, when he has laid a foundation, and is not able to finish, all who see it begin to mock him, saying, 'This man began to build, and was not able to finish.' Or what king, going to encounter another king in war, will not sit down first and take counsel whether he is able with ten thousand to meet him who comes against him with twenty thousand? And if not, while the other is yet a great way off, he sends an embassy and asks terms of peace. So therefore, whoever of you does not renounce all that he has cannot be my disciple." (*Luke 14:27–33*)

Key Ideas: Each person bears a cross
The cost of discipleship
The wisdom in commitment

Action Step: Make a chart of your Christian fellowship suggesting the diversity of directions Christian responsibility takes in the world beyond the sanctuary.

Prayer: Lord, if I am able to bear my cross today it will only be because You have given me a vision that my being a disciple of the Christ is worth every sacrifice that is required.

78 GOD'S SEARCHING LOVE

So he told them this parable: "What man of you, having a hundred sheep, if he has lost one of them, does not leave the ninety-nine in the wilderness, and go after the one which is lost, until he finds it? And when he has found it, he lays it on his shoulders, rejoicing. And when he comes home, he calls together his friends and his neighbors, saying to them, 'Rejoice with me, for I have found my sheep which was lost.' Even so, I tell you, there will be more joy in heaven over one sinner who repents than over ninety-nine righteous persons who need no repentance." *(Luke 15:3–7)*

Key Ideas: The worth of one wandering soul
The results of searching love
The joy of heaven on earth

Action Step: Contact one person you know who is living on the edge of your community life; show him or her your genuine concern.

Prayer: Help me, Lord, to reach out today with a person-minded interest in the lonely and the lost.

79 GOD'S PATIENT LOVE

But when he came to himself he said, "How many of my father's hired servants have bread enough and to spare, but I perish here with hunger! I will arise and go to my father, and I will say to him, 'Father, I have sinned against heaven and before you; I am no longer worthy to be called your son; treat me as one of your hired servants.' " And he arose and came to his father. But while he was yet at a distance, his father saw him and had compassion, and ran and embraced him and kissed him. And the son said to him, "Father, I have sinned against heaven and before you; I am no longer worthy to be called your son." But the father said to his servants, "Bring quickly the best robe, and put it on him; and put a ring on his hand, and shoes on his feet; and bring the fatted calf and kill it, and let us eat and make merry; for this my son was dead, and is alive again; he was lost, and is found." And they began to make merry. *(Luke 15:17–24)*

Key Ideas: A son who woke up
A father who kept waiting
A celebration of new life

Action Step: Plan some community or church dialogues with young people, parents, and other adults around the theme: "Free to be me—with my parents, my peers, the larger society, and God."

Prayer: Keep me dissatisfied today, Lord, if I settle for anything less than full partnership in Your creation and responsibility with the freedom You continually give to me.

80 CHALLENGE TO COMPASSION

"There was a rich man, who was clothed in purple and fine linen and who feasted sumptuously every day. At his gate lay a poor man named Lazarus, full of sores, who desired to be fed with what fell from the rich man's table; moreover the dogs came and licked his sores. The poor man died and was carried by the angels to Abraham's bosom. The rich man also died and was buried; and in Hades, being in torment, he lifted up his eyes, and saw Abraham far off and Lazarus in his bosom. And he called out, 'Father Abraham, have mercy upon me, and send Lazarus to dip the end of his finger in water and cool my tongue; for I am in anguish in this flame.' But Abraham said, 'Son, remember that you in your lifetime received your good things, and Lazarus in like manner evil things; but now he is comforted here, and you are in anguish. And besides all this, between us and you a great chasm has been fixed, in order that those who would pass from here to you may not be able, and none may cross from there to us.' " (*Luke 16:19–26*)

Key Ideas: Food and health are wealth
Need at our doorstep
The great divide

Action Step: Seek out the facts about the hungry peoples of the world—at home and around the globe—the causes and steps toward the solution of this human dilemma.

Prayer: Lord, move me today beyond guilt feelings about starving people to involvement in some worthwhile projects of caring.

81 KEEP ON FORGIVING

And he said to his disciples, "Temptations to sin are sure to come; but woe to him by whom they come! It would be better for him if a millstone were hung round his neck and he were cast into the sea, then that he should cause one of these little ones to sin. Take heed to yourselves; if your brother sins, rebuke him, and if he repents, forgive him; and if he sins against you seven times in the day, and turns to you seven times, and says, 'I repent,' you must forgive him." *(Luke 17:1–4)*

Key Ideas: Tempting others endangers all
Believe others can change
Uncalculating forgiveness

Action Step: Be willing to give a second chance to someone who makes a mistake, remembering how others have helped you.

Prayer: Strengthen me, Lord, when I should forgive another today.

82 THE SPIRIT OF SERVICE

"Will any one of you, who has a servant plowing or keeping sheep, say to him when he has come in from the field, 'Come at once and sit down at table?' Will he not rather say to him, 'Prepare supper for me, and gird yourself and serve me, till I eat and drink; and afterward you shall eat and drink'? Does he thank the servant because he did what was commanded? So you also, when you have done all that is commanded you, say, 'We are unworthy servants; we have only done what was our duty.' " *(Luke 17:7–10)*

Key Ideas: Opportunity to serve
Obligations as well as benefits
Obedience never ends

Action Step: Show someone the meaning of unmerited grace by inviting them to do something for which it will be impossible for them to repay you.

Prayer: It is a thrilling thought for me today, Lord, knowing Your limitless love for this gigantic world and even for me.

83 THE RESURRECTION AND THE LIFE

Now when Jesus came, he found that Lazarus had already been in the tomb four days. Bethany was near Jerusalem, about two miles off, and many of the Jews had come to Martha and Mary to console them concerning their brother. When Martha heard that Jesus was coming, she went and met him, while Mary sat in the house. Martha said to Jesus, "Lord, if you had been here, my brother would not have died. And even now I know that whatever you ask from God, God will give you." Jesus said to her, "Your brother will rise again." Martha said to him, "I know that he will rise again in the resurrection at the last day." Jesus said to her, "I am the resurrection and the life; he who believes in me though he die, yet shall he live, and whoever lives and believes in me shall never die. Do you believe this?" She said to him, "Yes, Lord; I believe that you are the Christ, the Son of God, he who is coming into the world." (*John 11:17–27*)

Key Ideas: Jesus stood by His friends
Jesus had hope to share
Jesus is God's hope personalized

Action Step: Together with your minister and other interested persons reflect on the purpose and principles of a Christian memorial and burial service; offer these as guidelines to the rest of your church.

Prayer: Lord, I am upheld today with the consolation that there is no depth of grief and personal loss that You cannot pull me through.

84 SAYING "THANK YOU"

On the way to Jerusalem he was passing along between Samaria and Galilee. And as he entered a village, he was met by ten lepers, who stood at a distance and lifted up their voices and said, "Jesus, Master, have mercy on us." When he saw them he said to them, "Go and show yourselves to the priests." And as they went they were cleansed. Then one of them, when he saw that he was healed, turned back, praising God with a loud voice; and he fell on his face at Jesus' feet, giving him thanks. Now he was a Samaritan. Then said Jesus, "Were not ten cleansed? Where are the nine? Was no one found to return and give praise to God except this foreigner?" And he said to him, "Rise and go your way; your faith has made you well." (*Luke 17:11–19*)

Key Ideas: Sick people seek a physician
Thanksgiving is a decision
Our enemies can teach us

Action Step: Whoever you are prejudiced against make an effort to meet them with new compassion.

Prayer: Today, Lord, I rejoice and give thanks to You without hesitation or reservation.

85 LOCATING THE KINGDOM

Being asked by the Pharisees when the kingdom of God was coming, he answered them, "The kingdom of God is not coming with signs to be observed; nor will they say, 'Lo, here it is!' or 'There!' for behold, the kingdom of God is in the midst of you." (*Luke 17:20, 21*)

Key Ideas: Hope of the coming Kingdom
How the Kingdom is not coming
Here is the Kingdom

Action Step: Share with your family or immediate friends how you can see God in genuine loving interpersonal communications.

Prayer: Lord, help me to express my faith today in words growing out of my own personal experience.

86 HUMILITY BEFORE GOD

He also told this parable to some who trusted in themselves that they were righteous and despised others: "Two men went up into the temple to pray, one a Pharisee and the other a tax collector. The Pharisee stood and prayed thus with himself, 'God, I thank thee that I am not like other men, extortioners, unjust, adulterers, or even like this tax collector. I fast twice a week, I give tithes of all that I get.' But the tax collector, standing far off, would not even lift up his eyes to heaven, but beat his breast, saying, 'God, be merciful to me a sinner!' I tell you, this man went down to his house justified rather than the other; for every one who exalts himself will be humbled, but he who humbles himself will be exalted." (*Luke 18:9–14*)

Key Ideas: The danger of being religious
The cry of the down-and-out
Success in God's eyes

Action Step: Speak lovingly and honestly to a discouraged and weakened neighbor or friend about your own struggles.

Prayer: Lord, without Your continual forgiveness I will not be able to go forward today when I fall short of being as good as the Christ calls me to be.

87 GOD'S GIFT OF MARRIAGE

"But from the beginning of creation, 'God made them male and female.' 'For this reason a man shall leave his father and mother and be joined to his wife, and the two shall become one flesh.' So they are no longer two but one flesh. What therefore God has joined together, let not man put asunder." (*Mark 10:6–9*)

Key Ideas: The divine ideal of family
The strange mathematics of marriage
The covenant is for life

Action Step: Push for a regular continuing course in "marriage and the family" in an upper grade in your school system.

Prayer: Lord, I feel a challenge today from many couples whose healthy and enduring marriages have shown me how to live.

88 THE CHILD SPIRIT

And they were bringing children to him, that he might touch them; and the disciples rebuked them. But when Jesus saw it he was indignant, and said to them, "Let the children come to me, do not hinder them; for to such belongs the kingdom of God. Truly, I say to you, whoever does not receive the kingdom of God like a child shall not enter it." And he took them in his arms and blessed them, laying his hands upon them. (*Mark 10:13–16*)

Key Ideas: Hoping for Jesus' touch
Children always welcome
The Kingdom spirit

Action Step: Offer your services—teaching, helping, counseling, encouraging—in some area of your congregation's work with children and youth.

Prayer: Lord, today I will seek to learn from every child I see and meet.

89 REWARDS FROM GOD

And Jesus looked around and said to his disciples, "How hard it will be for those who have riches to enter the kingdom of God!" And the disciples were amazed at his words. But Jesus said to them again, "Children, how hard it is to enter the kingdom of God! It is easier for a camel to go through the eye of a needle than for a rich man to enter the kingdom of God." And they were exceedingly astonished, and said to him, "Then who can be saved?" Jesus looked at them and said, "With men it is impossible, but not with God; for all things are possible with God." Peter began to say to him, "Lo, we have left everything and followed you." Jesus said, "Truly, I say to you, there is no one who has left house or brothers or sisters or mother or father or children or lands, for my sake and for the gospel, who will not receive a hundredfold now in this time, houses and brothers and sisters and mothers and children and lands, with persecutions, and in the age to come eternal life." (*Mark 10:23–30*)

Key Ideas: The peril of prosperity
The God of the impossible
The Christian's larger family

Action Step: In a family conference ask the question; "What would we have to hold us together if we lost all our possessions by fire, flood, tornado, or earthquake?"

Prayer: You and I alone know today, Lord, how much of my material wealth should be in the service of Your Kingdom.

90 GREAT THROUGH SERVICE

And they said to him, "Grant us to sit, one at your right hand and one at your left, in your glory." But Jesus said to them, "You do not know what you are asking. Are you able to drink the cup that I drink, or to be baptized with the baptism with which I am baptized?" And they said to him, "We are able." And Jesus said to them, "The cup that I drink you will drink; and with the baptism with which I am baptized, you will be baptized; but to sit at my right hand or at my left is not mine to grant, but it is for those for whom it has been prepared." And when the ten heard it, they began to be indignant at James and John. And Jesus called them to him and said to them, "You know that those who are supposed to rule over the Gentiles lord it over them, and their great men exercise authority over them. But it shall not be so among you; but whoever would be great among you must be your servant, and whoever would be first among you must be slave of all. For the Son of man also came not to be served but to serve, and to give his life as a ransom for many." (*Mark 10:37–45*)

Key Ideas: The search for special privilege
The sacrament of suffering
The superior way of service

Action Step: Deliberately assume a position or accept a task in your Christian fellowship that will require work and service to others.

Prayer: Lord, only with Your help today will I be able to labor hard for others with little or no public recognition.

91 THE SURPRISE INVITATION

He entered Jericho and was passing through. And there was a man named Zacchaeus; he was a chief tax collector, and rich. And he sought to see who Jesus was, but could not, on account of the crowd, because he was small of stature. So he ran on ahead and climbed up into a sycamore tree to see him, for he was to pass that way. And when Jesus came to the place, he looked up and said to him, "Zacchaeus, make haste and come down; for I must stay at your house today." So he made haste and came down, and received him joyfully. And when they saw it they all murmured, "He has gone in to be the guest of a man who is a sinner." And Zacchaeus stood and said to the Lord, "Behold, Lord, the half of my goods I give to the poor; and if I have defrauded any one of anything, I restore it fourfold." And Jesus said to him, "Today salvation has come to this house, since he also is a son of Abraham. For the Son of man came to seek and to save that which was lost." (*Luke 19:1–10*)

Key Ideas: On the lookout for Jesus
At the table with Jesus
Discovering salvation from Jesus

Action Step: Take the initiative to plan an occasion for an informal, friendly conversation with an individual or family within your reach who needs a new way of living.

Prayer: Lord, You have begun a revolution in my life today, and I may never be the same again!

92 THE TRIUMPHAL ENTRY

And they brought the colt to Jesus, and threw their garments on it; and he sat upon it. And many spread their garments on the road, and others spread leafy branches which they had cut from the fields. And those who went before and those who followed cried out, "Hosanna! Blessed be he who comes in the name of the Lord! Blessed be the kingdom of our father David that is coming! Hosanna in the highest!" *(Mark 11:7–10)*

Key Ideas: Messiah on a donkey
Welcome by the people
God's Deliverer is here

Action Step: There will be some public demonstration or witness to the Christian faith in your community (parade float, fair booth, TV program, a cause to stand up for or carry a banner for); volunteer and experience making a public and visible witness to your belief.

Prayer: Lord, I will gladly be in the parade of praise for the Christ today.

93 TRESPASSING IN THE TEMPLE

And Jesus entered the temple of God and drove out all who sold and bought in the temple, and he overturned the tables of the money-changers and the seats of those who sold pigeons. He said to them, "It is written, 'My house shall be called a house of prayer'; but you make it a den of robbers." *(Matthew 21:12, 13)*

Key Ideas: Material in God's service
Spiritual house cleaning
Prophetic words about prayer

Action Step: Make an inventory of your church, not just its building and equipment, but also its programs, mission, and utilization of the building for the service of God and the community.

Prayer: Lord, forgive me today if I take for granted anything about Your Church.

94 A GRAIN FALLS AND DIES

"Truly, truly, I say to you, unless a grain of wheat falls into the earth and dies, it remains alone; but if it dies, it bears much fruit. He who loves his life loses it, and he who hates his life in this world will keep it for eternal life. If any one serves me, he must follow me; and where I am, there shall my servant be also; if any one serves me, the Father will honor him." (*John 12:24–26*)

Key Ideas: Life through sacrifice
A radical reversal of rewards
Serving Christ's way

Action Step: Plant some seeds with children at home, school, or church; watch the seeds bring new life in their own dying.

Prayer: I am slowly learning, Lord, that if I wish to do one thing well today, I must forsake many other good things.

95 CHRIST'S MAGNETIC APPEAL

"Now is the judgment of this world, now shall the ruler of this world be cast out; and I, when I am lifted up from the earth, will draw all men to myself." He said this to show by what death he was to die. The crowd answered him, "We have heard from the law that the Christ remains forever. How can you say that the Son of man must be lifted up? Who is this Son of man?" Jesus said to them, "The light is with you for a little longer. Walk while you have the light, lest the darkness overtake you; he who walks in the darkness does not know where he goes. While you have the light, believe in the light, that you may become sons of light." (*John 12:31–36*)

Key Ideas: A crucial encounter with evil
The enduring Christ
Growing with the light

Action Step: Determine to do something with your life that is a fitting personal memorial to those persons in our time who, like the Christ, were unafraid of risking death in encountering evil.

Prayer: Keep me singing today, Lord, "We shall overcome" together with every person and group who loves the way of justice, peace, compassion, and freedom.

96 THE VINEYARD OF GOD

And he began to tell the people this parable: "A man planted a vineyard, and let it out to tenants, and went into another country for a long while. When the time came, he sent a servant to the tenants, that they should give him some of the fruit of the vineyard; but the tenants beat him, and sent him away empty-handed. And he sent another servant; him also they beat and treated shamefully, and sent him away empty-handed. And he sent yet a third; this one they wounded and cast out. Then the owner of the vineyard said, 'What shall I do? I will send my beloved son; it may be they will respect him.' But when the tenants saw him, they said to themselves, 'This is the heir; let us kill him, that the inheritance may be ours.' And they cast him out of the vineyard and killed him. What then will the owner of the vineyard do to them? He will come and destroy those tenants, and give the vineyard to others." When they heard this, they said, "God forbid!" But he looked at them and said, "What then is this that is written:

> The very stone which the builders rejected has become the head of the corner?

Every one who falls on that stone will be broken to pieces; but when it falls on any one it will crush him." (*Luke 20:9–18*)

Key Ideas: God is our Landlord
The call to accountability
Destruction or life?

Action Step: Join some effort to ensure that the public conserves and pro tects the land and quality of the environment.

Prayer: Lord, I will be slow today in turning away from courageous interpreters of our times who tell us hard facts about our society and earth.

97 GOD AND GOVERNMENTS

And they came and said to him, "Teacher, we know that you are true, and care for no man; for you do not regard the position of men, but truly teach the way of God. Is it lawful to pay taxes to Caesar, or not? Should we pay them, or should we not?" But knowing their hypocrisy, he said to them, "Why put me to the test? Bring me a coin, and let me look at it." And they brought one. And he said to them, "Whose likeness and inscription is this?" They said to him, "Caesar's." Jesus said to them, "Render to Caesar the things that are Caesar's, and to God the things that are God's." (*Mark 12:14–17*)

Key Ideas: Jesus deals with flattery
Answering a question with a question
Honor your leaders, but worship God

Action Step: While respecting the freedom of fellow citizens to be believers or nonbelievers, confidently interpret to others the religious roots of your national history and heritage.

Prayer: Give me common sense and courage today, Lord, to treasure my patriotic heritage within the larger context of Your kingly rule.

98 TWO GREAT COMMANDMENTS

And one of the scribes came up and heard them disputing with one another, and seeing that he answered them well, asked him, "Which commandment is the first of all?" Jesus answered, "The first is, 'Hear, O Israel: The Lord our God, the Lord is one; and you shall love the Lord your God with all your heart, and with all your soul, and with all your mind, and with all your strength.' The second is this, 'You shall love your neighbor as yourself.' There is no other commandment greater than these." (*Mark 12:28–31*)

Key Ideas: Christ, the master Teacher
The highest goal of love
The farthest reaches of love

Action Step: Memorize these two basic principles as guidelines for making Christian decisions in every area of your life.

Prayer: Lord, with Your help today I am going to concentrate on the kind of love that enriches all of life.

99 TITHING AND MORE

"Woe to you, scribes and Pharisees, hypocrites! for you tithe mint and dill and cummin, and have neglected the weightier matters of the law, justice and mercy and faith; these you ought to have done, without neglecting the others. You blind guides, straining out a gnat and swallowing a camel!" (*Matthew 23:23, 24*)

Key Ideas: Religion of rules
Neglecting priorities
Blurred vision

Action Step: Occasionally in a committee or organizational meeting of your church ask the question, "What is the purpose of our group and this meeting?"

Prayer: Help me today, Lord, to sort out the significant from the superfluous.

100 CARING FOR A CITY

"O Jerusalem, Jerusalem, killing the prophets and stoning those who are sent to you! How often would I have gathered your children together as a hen gathers her brood under her wings, and you would not! Behold, your house is forsaken and desolate. For I tell you, you will not see me again, until you say, 'Blessed be he who comes in the name of the Lord.' " (*Matthew 23:37–39*)

Key Ideas: The unholy city
God's persistent love
Revelation accompanies affirmation

Action Step: Invite a public official in your city who is trying to build up the total good of your community to your church for an open forum.

Prayer: Lord, because of Your guidance I will not lose my way today.

101 THE SPIRIT OF STEWARDSHIP

He looked up and saw the rich putting their gifts into the treasury; and he saw a poor widow put in two copper coins. And he said, "Truly I tell you, this poor widow has put in more than all of them; for they all contributed out of their abundance, but she out of her poverty put in all the living that she had." (*Luke 21:1–4*)

Key Ideas: A spiritual habit with money
Jesus noticed the unspectacular
The strange logic of liberality

Action Step: Develop a way of giving recognition in your Christian fellowship to the sincere and dedicated financial stewardship of every individual and family.

Prayer: Lord, I will practice consistent stewardship and will not withhold myself in giving today.

102 THE DAY OF JUDGMENT

"But of that day and hour no one knows, not even the angels of heaven, nor the Son, but the Father only. As were the days of Noah, so will be the coming of the Son of man. For as in those days before the flood they were eating and drinking, marrying and giving in marriage, until the day when Noah entered the ark, and they did not know until the flood came and swept them all away, so will be the coming of the Son of man. Then two men will be in the field; one is taken and one is left. Two women will be grinding at the mill; one is taken and one is left. Watch therefore, for you do not know on what day your Lord is coming." (*Matthew 24:36–42*)

Key Ideas: The unknown within our certainty
Playing with the judgment of God
Everyone may not make it

Action Step: Show a friend or fellow worker how to take this life and the life that is to come seriously without ignoring his or her daily tasks.

Prayer: Today, Lord, I will live and work and play without forgetting this could be my last day in this flesh.

103 THE RISK OF FAITH

"Now after a long time the master of those servants came and settled accounts with them. And he who had received the five talents came forward, bringing five talents more, saying, 'Master, you delivered to me five talents; here I have made five talents more.' His master said to him, 'Well done, good and faithful servant; you have been faithful over a little, I will set you over much; enter into the joy of your master.' And he also who had the two talents came forward, saying, 'Master, you delivered to me two talents; here I have made two talents more.' His master said to him, 'Well done, good and faithful servant; you have been faithful over a little, I will set you over much; enter into the joy of your master.' He also who had received the one talent came forward, saying, 'Master, I knew you to be a hard man, reaping where you did not sow, and gathering where you did not winnow; so I was afraid, and I went and hid your talent in the ground. Here you have what is yours.' But his master answered him, 'You wicked and slothful servant! You knew that I reap where I have not sowed, and gather where I have not winnowed? Then you ought to have invested my money with the bankers, and at my coming I should have received what was my own with interest. So take the talent from him, and give it to him who has the ten talents. For to every one who has will more be given, and he will have abundance; but from him who has not, even what he has will be taken away." (*Matthew 25:19–29*)

Key Ideas: Superiority in stewardship
Making the average outstanding
Making the best of our opportunities

Action Step: Risk utilizing one of your talents in some new way, with a new group of persons, or in a new cause that deserves personal involvement.

Prayer: If I can know I am pleasing You, that will be enough satisfaction for me today, Lord.

104 THE COMPASSION TEST

"When the Son of man comes in his glory, and all the angels with him, then he will sit on his glorious throne. Before him will be gathered all the nations, and he will separate them one from another as a shepherd separates the sheep from the goats, and he will place the sheep at his right hand, but the goats at the left. Then the King will say to those at his right hand, 'Come, O blessed of my Father, inherit the kingdom prepared for you from the foundation of the world; for I was hungry and you gave me food, I was thirsty and you gave me drink, I was a stranger and you welcomed me, I was naked and you clothed me, I was sick and you visited me, I was in prison and you came to me.' Then the righteous will answer him, 'Lord, when did we see thee hungry and feed thee, or thirsty and give thee drink? And when did we see thee a stranger and welcome thee, or naked and clothe thee? And when did we see thee sick or in prison and visit thee?' And the King will answer them, 'Truly, I say to you, as you did it to one of the least of these my brethren, you did it to me.' " *(Matthew 25:31–40)*

Key Ideas: The universal judgment
Commendation of caring
Helping the hidden Christ

Action Step: Strategically plan a series of experiences for young people by which you may teach them how to care about suffering and troubled persons.

Prayer: Teach me today, Lord, to see Your face in the faces of strangers as well as my friends.

105 THE BEAUTY OF LOVE

Now when Jesus was at Bethany in the house of Simon the leper, a woman came up to him with an alabaster jar of very expensive ointment, and she poured it on his head, as he sat at table. But when the disciples saw it, they were indignant, saying, "Why this waste? For this ointment might have been sold for a large sum, and given to the poor." But Jesus, aware of this, said to them, "Why do you trouble the woman? For she has done a beautiful thing to me. For you always have the poor with you, but you will not always have me. In pouring this ointment on my body she has done it to prepare me for burial. Truly, I say to you, wherever this gospel is preached in the whole world, what this woman has done will be told in memory of her." *(Matthew 26:6–13)*

Key Ideas: The anointing of love
Economy fails by itself
Beneath surface appearances

Action Step: Take flowers or some other appropriate gift to someone you love or wish to make happy.

Prayer: Lord, one of my aims for living today is the appreciation of people who bless my life.

When he had washed their feet, and taken his garments, and resumed his place, he said to them, "Do you know what I have done to you? You call me Teacher and Lord; and you are right, for so I am. If I then, your Lord and Teacher, have washed your feet, you also ought to wash one another's feet. For I have given you an example, that you also should do as I have done to you. Truly, truly, I say to you, a servant is not greater than his master; nor is he who is sent greater than he who sent him." (*John 13:12–16*)

Key Ideas: Spirituality of towel and basin
Authority stoops to serve
Following our Leader, Christ

Action Step: Whatever the work within your reach, make a point of proving that you are not above others by doing your share willingly.

Prayer: Lord, help me to make some progress today in learning how to deserve opportunities to lead because of my faithful labors.

107 THE LABEL OF LOVE

"A new commandment I give to you, that you love one another; even as I have loved you, that you also love one another. By this all men will know that you are my disciples, if you have love for one another." (*John 13:34, 35*)

Key Ideas: A new commandment
A new standard of love
A new test of religion

Action Step: Transform your concern and good feelings for others into action; do something besides thinking or talking good thoughts; prove your love by caring for specific persons.

Prayer: Lord, I hope to be identified as a disciple of Christ today by the way I treat everyone I meet.

108 IN THE NEED OF PRAYER

"Simon, Simon, behold, Satan demanded to have you, that he might sift you like wheat, but I have prayed for you that your faith may not fail; and when you have turned again, strengthen your brethren." And he said to him, "Lord, I am ready to go with you to prison and to death." He said, "I tell you, Peter, the cock will not crow this day, until you three times deny that you know me." (*Luke 22:31–34*)

Key Ideas: Faith can fail
Reconversion and its proof
Pride goes before a fall

Action Step: Begin an aggressive but tactful recovery and rehabilitation program for Christian dropouts from your church.

Prayer: Today, Lord, I need Your aid, not just in keeping true to my faith but also in keeping it going.

109 THE LORD'S SUPPER

And as they were eating, he took bread, and blessed, and broke it, and gave it to them, and said, "Take; this is my body." And he took a cup, and when he had given thanks he gave it to them, and they all drank of it. And he said to them, "This is my blood of the covenant, which is poured out for many. Truly, I say to you, I shall not drink again of the fruit of the vine until that day when I drink it new in the kingdom of God." (*Mark 14:22–25*)

Key Ideas: The supper became a sacrament
The sign of the New Covenant
The signal of the Kingdom

Action Step: Covenant with Christ Jesus to go all the way in loyalty to Him even if it may mean giving up your own flesh and blood.

Prayer: Today, Lord, I am going to turn all meetings of persons and eating together with others into a sacrament because of Jesus.

110 MY FATHER'S HOUSE

"Let not your hearts be troubled; believe in God, believe also in me. In my Father's house are many rooms; if it were not so, would I have told you that I go to prepare a place for you? And when I go and prepare a place for you, I will come again and will take you to myself, that where I am you may be also. And you know the way where I am going." Thomas said to him, "Lord, we do not know where you are going; how can we know the way?" Jesus said to him, "I am the way, and the truth, and the life; no one comes to the Father, but by me." *(John 14:1–6)*

Key Ideas: The ground of our faith
Breakthrough beyond death
The key to fellowship with God

Action Step: Talk freely and frankly about your mortality with persons who are closest to you, especially your family.

Prayer: I cannot fear the threat of death, Lord, since today I am trusting in You.

111 GREATER WORKS

"Truly, truly, I say to you, he who believes in me will also do the works that I do; and greater works than these will he do, because I go to the Father. Whatever you ask in my name, I will do it, that the Father may be glorified in the Son; if you ask anything in my name, I will do it. If you love me, you will keep my commandments. And I will pray the Father, and he will give you another Counselor, to be with you forever, even the Spirit of truth, whom the world cannot receive, because it neither sees him nor knows him; you know him, for he dwells with you, and will be in you." *(John 14:12–17)*

Key Ideas: The expanding ministry of Christ
The prayer base of our ministry
The Master's prayer and promise

Action Step: Write some brief open-ended parables about churches with different predicaments, problems, and challenges; suggest that your church leaders share their conclusions and solutions.

Prayer: Lord, open my mind today toward creative imagination in devising new possibilities in accomplishing the tasks before me as a Christian.

112 THE SPIRIT HELPER

"These things I have spoken to you, while I am still with you. But the Counselor, the Holy Spirit, whom the Father will send in my name, he will teach you all things, and bring to your remembrance all that I have said to you. Peace I leave with you; my peace I give to you; not as the world gives do I give to you. Let not your hearts be troubled, neither let them be afraid." *(John 14:25–27)*

Key Ideas: The promise of the Holy Spirit
The mission of the Holy Spirit
The *shalom* of Christ

Action Step: Extend to persons you meet this day some sign or word of good wishes for their inward peace.

Prayer: Lord, I can live with some depth today because Your providence includes my soul and spirit as well as the needs of my physical body.

113 THE VINE AND BRANCHES

"Abide in me, and I in you. As the branch cannot bear fruit by itself, unless it abides in the vine, neither can you, unless you abide in me. I am the vine, you are the branches. He who abides in me, and I in him, he it is that bears much fruit, for apart from me you can do nothing. If a man does not abide in me, he is cast forth as a branch and withers; and the branches are gathered, thrown into the fire and burned. If you abide in me, and my words abide in you, ask whatever you will, and it shall be done for you. By this my Father is glorified, that you bear much fruit, and so prove to be my disciples. As the Father has loved me, so have I loved you; abide in my love. If you keep my commandments, you will abide in my love, just as I have kept my Father's commandments and abide in his love. These things I have spoken to you, that my joy may be in you, and that your joy may be full." *(John 15:4–11)*

Key Ideas: Staying close to Christ
A choice of withering or fruitfulness
Joy in obedience

Action Step: Take a good look at a house plant or a garden flower today; use your observations to write a parable.

Prayer: Lord, it is more important today that I walk with You as close as I know how even though I always expect You to walk closely with me.

114 FRIENDS WITH CHRIST

"Greater love has no man than this, that a man lay down his life for his friends. You are my friends if you do what I command you. No longer do I call you servants, for the servant does not know what his master is doing; but I have called you friends, for all that I have heard from my Father I have made known to you. You did not choose me, but I chose you and appointed you that you should go and bear fruit and that your fruit should abide; so that whatever you ask the Father in my name, he may give it to you. This I command you, to love one another." (*John 15:13–17*)

Key Ideas: The divine model of love
From servants to friends
Election for a purpose

Action Step: Seek the friendship of those individuals whose class, vocational situation, or position of authority and responsibility has in the past kept you from knowing them personally.

Prayer: While I need and appreciate the pleasures of friendship, Lord, I have mixed feelings today about my ability to pay the price of genuine friendships.

115 THE SPIRIT'S WORK

"When the Spirit of truth comes, he will guide you into all the truth; for he will not speak on his own authority, but whatever he hears he will speak, and he will declare to you the things that are to come. He will glorify me, for he will take what is mine and declare it to you." (*John 16:13, 14*)

Key Ideas: The promise of the Spirit
The authority of the Spirit
The aim of the Spirit

Action Step: Carry out tasks true to the Spirit of Christ, trusting that they will be "of the Spirit," whether or not there is a special spiritual feeling attending them.

Prayer: Lord, today may all of my spiritual "highs" and inspirations always be true to the Christ.

116 JOY IN SPITE OF TROUBLE

"Truly, truly, I say to you, you will weep and lament, but the world will rejoice; you will be sorrowful, but your sorrow will turn into joy. When a woman is in travail she has sorrow, because her hour has come; but when she is delivered of the child, she no longer remembers the anguish, for joy that a child is born into the world. So you have sorrow now, but I will see you again and your hearts will rejoice, and no one will take your joy from you. In that day you will ask nothing of me. Truly, truly, I say to you, if you ask anything of the Father, he will give it to you in my name. Hitherto you have asked nothing in my name; ask, and you will receive, that your joy may be full." *(John 16:20–24)*

Key Ideas: Temporary sorrow
Enduring joy
Great expectations

Action Step: Set some long-term goal or project for yourself or for your family that will require patience, saving, and personal effort before you can fully reap the rewards.

Prayer: Lord, You have given me today the hope of new tomorrows, and I will not allow my sorrows to break me.

117 PRAYER FOR UNITY

"I do not pray that thou shouldst take them out of the world, but that thou shouldst keep them from the evil one. They are not of the world, even as I am not of the world. Consecrate them in the truth; thy word is truth. As thou didst send me into the world, so I have sent them into the world. And for their sake I consecrate myself, that they also may be consecrated in truth. I do not pray for these only, but also for those who are to believe in me through their word, that they may all be one; even as thou, Father, are in me, and I in thee, that they also may be in us, so that the world may believe that thou hast sent me." *(John 17:15–21)*

Key Ideas: Some earthly good
In the circle of truth and love
Unity with a purpose

Action Step: Determine some basic human problem or crisis in your community or world; try to bring Christians of various denominations together for joint strategy and action.

Prayer: Today, Lord, I am restless because of the distrust and disunity among Christians that prevent the fulfillment of our common mission.

118 THE GARDEN OF PRAYER

Then Jesus went with them to a place called Gethsemane, and he said to his disciples, "Sit here, while I go yonder and pray." And taking with him Peter and the two sons of Zebedee, he began to be sorrowful and troubled. Then he said to them, "My soul is very sorrowful, even to death; remain here, and watch with me." And going a little farther he fell on his face and prayed, "My Father, if it be possible, let this cup pass from me; nevertheless, not as I will, but as thou wilt." And he came to the disciples and found them sleeping; and he said to Peter, "So, could you not watch with me one hour? Watch and pray that you may not enter into temptation; the spirit indeed is willing, but the flesh is weak." (*Matthew 26:36–41*)

Key Ideas: Jesus in the agony of prayer
The deeper alternatives of life
Spiritual sleeping sickness

Action Step: Review your daily and weekly activities; make time in your busy and varied life situations for intensive dialogue with God.

Prayer: Lord, I earnestly want to be alert and ready today for communion with You.

119 STRENGTH OF THE PEACEMAKER

And he came up to Jesus at once and said, "Hail, Master!" And he kissed him. Jesus said to him, "Friend, why are you here?" Then they came up and laid hands on Jesus and seized him. And behold, one of those who were with Jesus stretched out his hand and drew his sword, and struck the slave of the high priest, and cut off his ear. Then Jesus said to him, "Put your sword back into its place; for all who take the sword will perish by the sword." (*Matthew 26:49–52*)

Key Ideas: The betrayal of a Friend
The arrest of God's own Son
The wrong defense of Jesus

Action Step: Make time to read a good book or article, or to enter into a good discussion that applies the principles of Christ to the issues of our times.

Prayer: Lord, keep my thinking clear and cool today when I am inclined to defend the right with contradictory means.

120 THE KINGSHIP OF CHRIST

Pilate entered the praetorium again and called Jesus, and said to him, "Are you the King of the Jews?" Jesus answered, "Do you say this of your own accord, or did others say it to you about me?" Pilate answered, "Am I a Jew? Your own nation and the chief priests have handed you over to me; what have you done?" Jesus answered, "My kingship is not of this world; if my kingship were of this world, my servants would fight, that I might not be handed over to the Jews; but my kingship is not from the world." Pilate said to him, "So you are a king?" Jesus answered, "You say that I am a king. For this I was born, and for this I have come into the world, to bear witness to the truth. Every one who is of the truth hears my voice." Pilate said to him, "What is truth?" *(John 18:33–38)*

Key Ideas: A bewildered judge
In defense of the spiritual
Jesus' confession of His kingship

Action Step: Go forth to encounter the power people and power structures; do not yield false allegiance to men as if they were gods; with whatever means of communication necessary, let them know that you know they are human and limited.

Prayer: Lord, I ask today for a sincere life so that I may know and understand the truth whenever it is embodied in persons I meet.

121 THE CRIME OF INJUSTICE

When day came, the assembly of the elders of the people gathered together, both chief priests and scribes; and they led him away to their council, and they said, "If you are the Christ, tell us." But he said to them,

"If I tell you, you will not believe; and if I ask you, you will not answer. But from now on the Son of man shall be seated at the right hand of the power of God." And they all said, "Are you the Son of God, then?" And he said to them, "You say that I am." And they said, "What further testimony do we need? We have heard it ourselves from his own lips." Then the whole company of them arose, and brought him before Pilate. (*Luke 22:66–23:1*)

Key Ideas: Christ before the court
Critics of the Christ
Christ of no crime

Action Step: Attend a court trial if you have never been to one; consider the dilemmas the judge and jury face.

Prayer: Whatever happens today, Lord, I always intend to be fair to my fellow human being.

122 THE CROWD AND CHRIST

Now at the feast he used to release for them any one prisoner for whom they asked. And among the rebels in prison, who had committed murder in the insurrection, there was a man called Barabbas. And the crowd came up and began to ask Pilate to do as he was wont to do for them. And he answered them, "Do you want me to release for you the King of the Jews?" For he perceived that it was out of envy that the chief priests had delivered him up. But the chief priests stirred up the crowd to have him release for them Barabbas instead. And Pilate again said to them, "Then what shall I do with the man whom you call the King of the Jews?" And they cried out again, "Crucify him." And Pilate said to them, "Why, what evil has he done?" But they shouted all the more, "Crucify him." So Pilate, wishing to satisfy the crowd, released for them Barabbas; and having scourged Jesus, he delivered him to be crucified. (*Mark 15:6–15*)

Key Ideas: When the mob rules
Conspiracy in religious garments
The policy of pleasing the crowd

Action Step: Offer your personal encouragement to political leaders who have the courage to act in their best wisdom and not merely in easy agreement with the selfish interests of the people.

Prayer: Lord, deliver me today from unthinking conformity to what everybody else is doing.

123 "FATHER, FORGIVE THEM"

Two others also, who were criminals, were led away to be put to death with him. And when they came to the place which is called The Skull, there they crucified him, and the criminals, one on the right and one on the left. And Jesus said, "Father, forgive them; for they know not what they do." And they cast lots to divide his garments. And the people stood by, watching; but the rulers scoffed at him, saying, "He saved others; let him save himself, if he is the Christ of God, his Chosen One!" The soldiers also mocked him, coming up and offering him vinegar, and saying, "If you are the King of the Jews, save yourself!" There was also an inscription over him, "This is the King of the Jews." (*Luke 23:32–38*)

Key Ideas: Christ counted among criminals
Love conquers evil
Miracles are not always God's will

Action Step: Lend your influence and support to those organizations and proposals that will ensure reasonable and ready justice for all.

Prayer: Lord, today I am going to try to forgive others regardless of their sin against me, because of Your great love in Jesus Your Son.

124 THE HANDS OF GOD

One of the criminals who were hanged railed at him, saying, "Are you not the Christ? Save yourself and us!" But the other rebuked him, saying, "Do you not fear God, since you are under the same sentence of condemnation? And we indeed justly; for we are receiving the due reward of our deeds; but this man has done nothing wrong." And he said, "Jesus, remember me when you come into your kingdom." And he said to him, "Truly, I say to you, today you will be with me in Paradise." It was now about the sixth hour, and there was darkness over the whole land until the ninth hour, while the sun's light failed; and the curtain of the temple was torn in two. Then Jesus, crying with a loud voice, said, "Father, into thy hands I commit my spirit!" And having said this he breathed his last. Now when the centurion saw what had taken place, he praised God, and said,

"Certainly this man was innocent!" And all the multitudes who assembled to see the sight, when they saw what had taken place, returned home beating their breasts. And all his acquaintances and the women who had followed him from Galilee stood at a distance and saw these things. (*Luke 23:39–49*)

Key Ideas: Hope for the confessing sinner
A prayer of total trust
Witnesses to human injustice

Action Step: Try confronting and making an appeal to a careless youth about the final destiny of his or her wrong direction of living; if it is done in love, what can you lose?

Prayer: Today, Lord, let me offer to a struggling and despairing brother or sister the promise of Your forgiving and hope-filled love.

125 THE LONELINESS OF DYING

Now from the sixth hour there was darkness over all the land until the ninth hour. And about the ninth hour Jesus cried with a loud voice, "Eli, Eli, lama sabach-thani?" that is, "My God, my God, why hast thou forsaken me?" And some of the bystanders hearing it said, "This man is calling Elijah." And one of them at once ran and took a sponge, filled it with vinegar, and put it on a reed, and gave it to him to drink. But the others said, "Wait, let us see whether Elijah will come to save him." And Jesus cried again with a loud voice and yielded up his spirit. (*Matthew 27:45–50*)

Key Ideas: Jesus shared our struggle
Wondering about help from God
The human agony of the Christ

Action Step: Invite a nurse, doctor, chaplain, or your minister to share with your group or church their experiences with dying persons.

Prayer: Today, Lord, I give thanks for Your undying love and power even when my life is overwhelmed with dark despair.

126 STANDING BY WITH LOVE

Standing by the cross of Jesus were his mother, and his mother's sister, Mary the wife of Clopas, and Mary Magdalene. When Jesus saw his mother, and the disciple whom he loved standing near, he said to his mother, "Woman, behold your son!" Then he said to the disciple, "Behold your mother!" And from that hour the disciple took her to his own home. After this Jesus, knowing that all was now finished, said (to fulfill the scripture), "I thirst." A bowl full of vinegar stood there; so they put a sponge full of the vinegar on hyssop and held it to his mouth. When Jesus had received the vinegar, he said, "It is finished"; and he bowed his head and gave up his spirit. (*John 19:25–30*)

Key Ideas: Love with loyalty
Our larger family of faith
The sacrament of submission

Action Step: Find someone beyond your immediate family and invite them into a larger family experience of fun and fellowship with you.

Prayer: Lord, I am staying true to You and others today, no matter what.

127 BURIAL IN A GARDEN

After this Joseph of Arimathea, who was a disciple of Jesus, but secretly, for fear of the Jews, asked Pilate that he might take away the body of Jesus; and Pilate gave him leave. So he came and took away his body. Nicodemus also, who had at first come to him by night, came bringing a mixture of myrrh and aloes, about a hundred pounds weight. They took the body of Jesus, and bound it in linen cloths with the spices, as is the burial custom of the Jews. Now in the place where he was crucified there was a garden, and in the garden a new tomb where no one had ever been laid. So because of the Jewish day of Preparation, as the tomb was close at hand, they laid Jesus there. (*John 19:38–42*)

Key Ideas: A conspiracy of love
A friend to the end
A garden of waiting

Action Step: Stand by a friend in a difficult situation when many others are reluctant.

Prayer: I find comfort today, Lord, in knowing that every person deserves personal respect all the way unto death.

128 THE BEGINNING OF EASTER

But on the first day of the week, at early dawn, they went to the tomb, taking the spices which they had prepared. And they found the stone rolled away from the tomb, but when they went in they did not find the body. While they were perplexed about this, behold, two men stood by them in dazzling apparel; and as they were frightened and bowed their faces to the ground, the men said to them, "Why do you seek the living among the dead?" *(Luke 24:1–5)*

Key Ideas: The dawning of Easter
The empty tomb
The word of life

Action Step: Celebrate new life given to the world through Jesus Christ whether it be Easter or not.

Prayer: Lord, I will live today by the inspiration of the mystery of Your life and love that You have demonstrated to the world once and for all in the resurrection of Jesus the Christ.

129 HE LIVES!

And they were saying to one another, "Who will roll away the stone for us from the door of the tomb?" And looking up, they saw that the stone was rolled back—it was very large. And entering the tomb, they saw a young man sitting on the right side, dressed in a white robe; and they were amazed. And he said to them, "Do not be amazed; you seek Jesus of Nazareth, who was crucified. He has risen, he is not here; see the place where they laid him. But go, tell his disciples and Peter that he is going before you to Galilee; there you will see him, as he told you." And they went out and fled from the tomb; for trembling and astonishment had come upon them; and they said nothing to any one, for they were afraid. *(Mark 16:3–8)*

Key Ideas: God rolled the stone away
Christ always goes before us
The moment of fear and trembling

Action Step: Be prepared to respond to the living Christ, who has often been at work in the lives of others long before you have begun to deal with them.

Prayer: Lord, I cannot be casual about Your presence in my world today since meeting You is filled with potential beyond my greatest expectations.

130 THE GARDEN OF RESURRECTION

But Mary stood weeping outside the tomb, and as she wept she stooped to look into the tomb; and she saw two angels in white, sitting where the body of Jesus had lain, one at the head and one at the feet. They said to her, "Woman, why are you weeping?" She said to them, "Because they have taken away my Lord, and I do not know where they have laid him." Saying this, she turned around and saw Jesus standing, but she did not know that it was Jesus. Jesus said to her, "Woman, why are you weeping? Whom do you seek?" Supposing him to be the gardener, she said to him, "Sir, if you have carried him away, tell me where you have laid him, and I will take him away." Jesus said to her, "Mary." She turned and said to him in Hebrew, "Rabboni!" (which means Teacher). (*John 20:11–16*)

Key Ideas: Caring that counts
Christ incognito
Conversation that communicates

Action Step: Greet everyone today in such a way that they will know Jesus Christ is alive and that it is worthwhile to be alive.

Prayer: Show me the way, Lord, to meet persons today in the genuine spirit of Your love.

131 CHRIST ON THE OPEN ROAD

So they drew near to the village to which they were going; and he made as though he would go further, but they constrained him, saying, "Stay with us, for it is toward evening and the day is now far spent." So he went in to stay with them. When he was at table with them, he took the bread and blessed, and broke it, and gave it to them. And their eyes were opened and they recognized him; and he vanished out of their sight. They said to each other, "Did not our hearts burn within us while he talked to us on the road, while he opened to us the scriptures?" And they rose that same hour and returned to Jerusalem; and they found the eleven gathered together and those who were with them, who said, "The Lord has risen indeed, and has appeared to Simon!" Then they told what had happened on the road, and how he was known to them in the breaking of the bread. (*Luke 24:28–35*)

Key Ideas: Christ the Stranger
Christ the Interpreter
Christ the Companion

Action Step: Volunteer to be a part of a sermon seminar in which the minister is asked to preach from some difficult texts of the Bible.

Prayer: Today, I ask, Lord, that You open my eyes to discover deeper truths in the Scriptures.

132 MUTUAL MINISTRY OF FORGIVENESS

On the evening of that day, the first day of the week, the doors being shut where the disciples were, for fear of the Jews, Jesus came and stood among them and said to them, "Peace be with you." When he had said this, he showed them his hands and his side. Then the disciples were glad when they saw the Lord. Jesus said to them again, "Peace be with you. As the Father has sent me, even so I send you." And when he had said this, he breathed on them, and said to them, "Receive the Holy Spirit. If you forgive the sins of any, they are forgiven; if you retain the sins of any, they are retained." (*John 20:19–23*)

Key Ideas: The penetrating peace of Christ
Sent out with the Spirit
An awesome agreement

Action Step: Look up information on the twelve disciples of Jesus in a good Bible dictionary or commentary.

Prayer: Lord, when I remember today what Jesus did with eleven fearful disciples, I am determined to give thanks for those who respond to our next meeting even if they are few in number.

133 DOUBT DISSOLVED

Now Thomas, one of the twelve, called the Twin, was not with them when Jesus came. So the other disciples told him, "We have seen the Lord." But he said to them, "Unless I see in his hands the print of the nails, and place my finger in the mark of the nails, and place my hand in his side, I will not believe." Eight days later, his disciples were again in the house, and Thomas was with them. The doors were shut, but Jesus came and stood among them, and said, "Peace be with you." Then he said to

Thomas, "Put your finger here, and see my hands; and put out your hand, and place it in my side; do not be faithless, but believing." Thomas answered him, "My Lord and my God!" (*John 20:24–28*)

Key Ideas: An inquiring disciple
The evidence for believing
Belief is commitment

Action Step: In a nonjudgmental way enter into a conversation with someone who is wrestling with real questions about the Christian faith; if the opportunity arises explain how you are dealing with these difficulties.

Prayer: Lord, I rest today in Your great love that can stand up to my deepest doubts and questions.

134 QUESTIONS OF COMMITMENT

When they had finished breakfast, Jesus said to Simon Peter, "Simon, son of John, do you love me more than these?" He said to him, "Yes, Lord; you know that I love you." He said to him, "Feed my lambs." A second time he said to him, "Simon, son of John, do you love me?" He said to him, "Yes, Lord; you know that I love you." He said to him, "Tend my sheep." He said to him the third time, "Simon, son of John, do you love me?" Peter was grieved because he said to him the third time, "Do you love me?" And he said to him, "Lord, you know everything; you know that I love you." Jesus said to him, "Feed my sheep." (*John 21:15–17*)

Key Ideas: The question of deeper loyalty
The confession of personal allegiance
The commission to care

Action Step: Offer to work alongside a new or younger Christian in some new responsibility that they have recently assumed.

Prayer: Today, Lord, I cannot forget those special people who have nurtured me intellectually, emotionally, and physically.

135 THE GREAT COMMISSION

Now the eleven disciples went to Galilee, to the mountain to which Jesus had directed them. And when they saw him they worshiped him; but some doubted. And Jesus came and said to them, "All authority in heaven and on earth has been given to me. Go therefore and make disciples of all nations, baptizing them in the name of the Father and of the Son and of the Holy Spirit, teaching them to observe all that I have commanded you; and lo, I am with you always, to the close of the age." (*Matthew 28:16–20*)

Key Ideas: All authority
All nations
Always

Action Step: Find a way to encourage your parish or Christian fellowship in its efforts to fulfill its evangelistic program and mission.

Prayer: Yes, Lord, I am going forth into the world today accepting Your assignment.

136 THE PROMISE OF POWER

"Thus it is written, that the Christ should suffer and on the third day rise from the dead, and that repentance and forgiveness of sins should be preached in his name to all nations, beginning from Jerusalem. You are witnesses of these things. And behold, I send the promise of my Father upon you; but stay in the city, until you are clothed with power from on high." (*Luke 24:46–49*)

Key Ideas: God's purpose in Jesus Christ
Good News for the nations
Power for our mission

Action Step: Review the message of the Good News about Jesus in the Gospels; reflect on the essential features of Jesus' life and their meaning to those to whom we bear witness.

Prayer: Lord, I do my activities today "in His name."

137 WITNESSES WITH POWER

"But you shall receive power when the Holy Spirit has come upon you; and you shall be my witnesses in Jerusalem and in all Judea and Samaria and to the end of the earth." (*Acts 1:8*)

Key Ideas: The promised power
The source of the power
The propulsion of the power

Action Step: Talk with some of your friends about the qualities of a Spirit-filled life that will empower persons for courageous and authentic witnessing.

Prayer: Lord, I will think big today, but I can't do it alone.

But Peter, standing with the eleven, lifted up his voice and addressed them, "Men of Judea and all who dwell in Jerusalem, let this be known to you, and give ear to my words. For these men are not drunk, as you suppose, since it is only the third hour of the day; but this is what was spoken by the prophet Joel:

> And in the last days it shall be, God declares,
> that I will pour out my Spirit upon all flesh,
> and your sons and your daughters shall prophesy,
> and your young men shall see visions,
> and your old men shall dream dreams;
> yea, and on my menservants and my maidservants in those days
> I will pour out my Spirit, and they shall prophesy.
> And I will show wonders in the heaven above
> and signs on the earth beneath,
> Blood, and fire, and vapor of smoke;
> the sun shall be turned into darkness
> and the moon into blood,
> before the day of the Lord comes,
> the great and manifest day.
> And it shall be that whoever calls on the name of the Lord shall be saved.

(Acts 2:14–21)

Key Ideas: In defense of enthusiasm
The Spirit is for all
A way to meet Judgment Day

Action Step: Keep in contact with the community of faith and be ready to stand up publicly to witness for your faith in Christ.

Prayer: Lord, free me today from careless disregard of men and women who are receiving new visions and dreams from You.

"Let all the house of Israel therefore know assuredly that God has made him both Lord and Christ, this Jesus whom you crucified." Now when they heard this they were cut to the heart, and said to Peter and the rest of the apostles, "Brethren, what shall we do?" And Peter said to them, "Repent, and be baptized every one of you in the name of Jesus Christ for the forgiveness of your sins; and you shall receive the gift of the Holy Spirit. For the promise is to you and to your children and to all that are far off, every one whom the Lord our God calls to him." And he testified with many other words and exhorted them, saying, "Save yourselves from this crooked generation." So those who received his word were baptized, and there were added that day about three thousand souls. And they devoted themselves to the apostles' teaching and fellowship, to the breaking of bread and the prayers. And fear came upon every soul; and many wonders and signs were done through the apostles. And all who believed were together and had all things in common; and they sold their possessions and goods and distributed them to all, as any had need. And day by day, attending the temple together and breaking bread in their homes, they partook of food with glad and generous hearts, praising God and having favor with all the people. And the Lord added to their number day by day those who were being saved. (*Acts 2:36–47*)

Key Ideas: Repentance makes the difference
Baptism visualizes our faith
Fellowship keeps us growing

Action Step: Explain to your non-Christian friends the reasons why Christians have practiced the rite of baptism as the door to vital incorporation into the Christian community of faith.

Prayer: Lord, today I hope to be a part of those believers whose celebrative and caring lifestyle demonstrates the true meaning of salvation.

140 MORE THAN MONEY

Now Peter and John were going up to the temple at the hour of prayer, the ninth hour. And a man lame from birth was being carried, whom they laid daily at that gate of the temple which is called Beautiful to ask alms of those who entered the temple. Seeing Peter and John about to go into the temple, he asked for alms. And Peter directed his gaze at him, with John, and said, "Look at us." And he fixed his attention upon them, expecting to receive something from them. But Peter said, "I have no silver and gold, but I give you what I have; in the name of Jesus Christ of Nazareth, walk." And he took him by the right hand and raised him up; and immediately his feet and ankles were made strong. And leaping up he stood and walked and entered the temple with them, walking and leaping and praising God. (*Acts 3:1–8*)

Key Ideas: On life's sidelines
Unexpected help
Joy abounding

Action Step: Carry out some helping project—personally or as a congregation—demonstrating that Christlike concern is more than simply monetary assistance.

Prayer: I will offer my prayers to You today, Lord, with my eyes wide open to the world of people and the human struggle.

141 CHRIST OUR SALVATION

And when they had set them in the midst, they inquired, "By what power or by what name did you do this?" Then Peter, filled with the Holy Spirit, said to them, "Rulers of the people and elders, if we are being examined today concerning a good deed done to a cripple, by what means this man has been healed, be it known to you all, and to all the people of Israel, that by the name of Jesus Christ of Nazareth, whom you crucified, whom God raised from the dead, by him this man is standing before you well. This is the stone which was rejected by you builders, but which has become the head of the corner. And there is salvation in no one else, for there is no other name under heaven given among men by which we must be saved." (*Acts 4:7–12*)

Key Ideas: Trying to stop Christianity
Acting in His name
An apologetic defense

Action Step: Among the several persons you may meet this day, look for opportunities to talk enthusiastically about the Good News of Jesus our Christ.

Prayer: Lord, make me an exclamation point of faith for all whom I meet today.

"What shall we do with these men? For that a notable sign has been performed through them is manifest to all the inhabitants of Jerusalem, and we cannot deny it. But in order that it may spread no further among the people, let us warn them to speak no more to any one in this name." So they called them and charged them not to speak or teach at all in the name of Jesus. But Peter and John answered them, "Whether it is right in the sight of God to listen to you rather than to God, you must judge; for we cannot but speak of what we have seen and heard." (*Acts 4:16–20*)

Key Ideas: Christian compassion becomes a threat
Understanding Christian commitment
The basis of Christian boldness

Action Step: Spend some time with older youth thinking through values and ways of acquiring values that supply strength of character within one's deepest self.

Prayer: Lord, prepare me today by small acts of courage in order that I may be ready when I am confronted with greater tests of my loyalty to You.

143 SHARING RESPONSIBILITY

Now in these days when the disciples were increasing in number, the Hellenists murmured against the Hebrews because their widows were neglected in the daily distribution. And the twelve summoned the body of the disciples and said, "It is not right that we should give up preaching the word of God to serve tables. Therefore, brethren, pick out from among you seven men of good repute, full of the Spirit and of wisdom, whom we may appoint to this duty. But we will devote ourselves to prayer and to the ministry of the word." (*Acts 6:1–4*)

Key Ideas: Added stress with success
The major ministry with God's Word
The spiritual ministry of compassion

Action Step: If you have allowed yourself to become overburdened, then risk requesting assistance and delegating work to others.

Prayer: Lord, give me the grace of heart today to respect and encourage the commitment and competence of my co-workers.

144 FIRST CHRISTIAN MARTYR

Now when they heard these things they were enraged, and they ground their teeth against him. But he, full of the Holy Spirit, gazed into heaven and saw the glory of God, and Jesus standing at the right hand of God; and he said, "Behold, I see the heavens opened, and the Son of man standing at the right hand of God." But they cried out with a loud voice and stopped their ears and rushed together upon him. Then they cast him out of the city and stoned him; and the witnesses laid down their garments at the feet of a young man named Saul. And as they were stoning Stephen, he prayed, "Lord Jesus, receive my spirit." And he knelt down and cried with a loud voice, "Lord, do not hold this sin against them." (*Acts 7:54–60*)

Key Ideas: The trinity of Christian confidence
Anger turned to hate
The courage of nonretaliation

Action Step: Consider lending your personal and financial support to an organization or cause following the principles of nonviolent reconciliation and encounter.

Prayer: Lord, I want to be able to live, give of myself, and forgive others today as one who can freely admit vulnerability with courage and trust in Your great purpose for the world.

145 KNOWING OUR FAITH

And the Spirit said to Philip, "Go up and join this chariot." So Philip ran to him, and heard him reading Isaiah the prophet, and asked, "Do you understand what you are reading?" And he said, "How can I, unless some one guides me?" And he invited Philip to come up and sit with him. Now the passage of the scripture which he was reading was this:

> As a sheep led to the slaughter
> or a lamb before its shearer is dumb,
> so he opens not his mouth.
> In his humiliation justice was denied him.
> Who can describe his generation?
> For his life is taken up from the earth.

And the eunuch said to Philip, "About whom, pray, does the prophet say this, about himself or about some one else?" Then Philip opened his mouth, and beginning with this scripture he told him the good news of Jesus. And as they went along the road they came to some water, and the eunuch said, "See, here is water! What is to prevent my being baptized?" And he commanded the chariot to stop, and they both went down into the water, Philip and the eunuch, and he baptized him. And when they came up out of the water, the Spirit of the Lord caught up Philip; and the eunuch saw him no more, and went on his way rejoicing. (*Acts 8:29–39*)

Key Ideas: Available to the Spirit
The Good News is Jesus
The joy of being baptized

Action Step: Begin a study of the "suffering Servant" in Isaiah, chapters 40 through 55, looking for prophecies concerning Jesus in His ministry as the Messiah.

Prayer: Lord, enroll me today in the apostolic order of "each one teach one."

AGENTS OF CONVERSION

Now there was a disciple at Damascus named Ananias. The Lord said to him in a vision, "Ananias." And he said, "Here I am, Lord." And the Lord said to him, "Rise and go to the street called Straight, and inquire in the house of Judas for a man of Tarsus named Saul; for behold, he is praying, and he has seen a man named Ananias come in and lay his hands on him so that he might regain his sight." But Ananias answered, "Lord, I have heard from many about this man, how much evil he has done to thy saints at Jerusalem; and here he has authority from the chief priests to bind all who call upon thy name." But the Lord said to him, "Go, for he is a chosen instrument of mine to carry my name before the Gentiles and kings and the sons of Israel; for I will show him how much he must suffer for the sake of my name." So Ananias departed and entered the house. And laying his hands on him he said, "Brother Saul, the Lord Jesus who appeared to you on the road by which you came, has sent me that you may regain your sight and be filled with the Holy Spirit." And immediately something like scales fell from his eyes and he regained his sight. Then he rose and was baptized, and took food and was strengthened. (*Acts 9:10–19*)

Key Ideas: On difficult assignment
Mediating God's Word
Believing is seeing anew

Action Step: In spite of the anticipated difficulties, risk conversing with someone with outstanding abilities about using his or her other talents in the service of Jesus the Christ.

Prayer: Today, Lord, I am filled with tears over deep feelings of thanksgiving for those who have loved and challenged me along my stumbling way.

147 INSPIRATIONS IN PRAYER

The next day, as they were on their journey and coming near the city, Peter went up on the housetop to pray, about the sixth hour. And he became hungry and desired something to eat; but while they were preparing it, he fell into a trance and saw the heaven opened, and something descending, like a great sheet, let down by four corners upon the earth. In it were all kinds of animals and reptiles and wild birds. And there came a voice to him, "Rise, Peter; kill and eat." But Peter said, "No, Lord; for I have never eaten anything that is common or unclean." And the voice came to him again a second time, "What God has cleansed, you must not call common." (*Acts 10:9–15*)

Key Ideas: The habit of prayer
Visions from our conscience
God speaks to us in prayer

Action Step: Shut down all of your frantic scheduling and activities on a day off; rest, relax, think, dream, and catch up on the free flow of imaginative alternatives for living.

Prayer: Lord, I will try today not to close off inspirations and visions of new truth from You.

148 GOD'S ACCEPTING LOVE

And Peter opened his mouth and said: "Truly I perceive that God shows no partiality, but in every nation any one who fears him and does what is right is acceptable to him. You know the word which he sent to Israel, preaching good news of peace by Jesus Christ (he is Lord of all), the word which was proclaimed throughout all Judea, beginning from Galilee after the baptism which John preached: how God anointed Jesus of Nazareth with the Holy Spirit and with power; how he went about doing good and healing all that were oppressed by the devil, for God was with him. And we are witnesses to all that he did both in the country of the Jews and in

Jerusalem. They put him to death by hanging him on a tree; but God raised him on the third day and made him manifest, not to all the people but to us who were chosen by God as witnesses, who ate and drank with him after he rose from the dead. And he commanded us to preach to the people, and to testify that he is the one ordained by God to be judge of the living and the dead. To him all the prophets bear witness that every one who believes in him receives forgiveness of sins through his name." (*Acts 10:34–43*)

Key Ideas: The Gospel of God's Peacemaker
The Gospel of God's Goodness
The Gospel of God's Victorious One

Action Step: Help your church become aware of some of the robust and realistic art of Jesus, the strong Son of God.

Prayer: Today, Lord, I too will be a witness to the Jesus of history, who is the Christ of my faith.

149 OUR UNIVERSAL NAME

And the hand of the Lord was with them, and a great number that believed turned to the Lord. News of this came to the ears of the church in Jerusalem, and they sent Barnabas to Antioch. When he came and saw the grace of God, he was glad; and he exhorted them all to remain faithful to the Lord with steadfast purpose; for he was a good man, full of the Holy Spirit and of faith. And a large company was added to the Lord. So Barnabas went to Tarsus to look for Saul; and when he had found him, he brought him to Antioch. For a whole year they met with the church, and taught a large company of people; and in Antioch the disciples were for the first time called Christians. (*Acts 11:21–26*)

Key Ideas: Success with intercultural Christianity
Co-ministers for Jesus Christ
The disciples are called *Christians*

Action Step: Evaluate the national, racial, and cultural groups in your community or Christian fellowship; recommend steps whereby these human diversities may be welcomed into one brotherhood in Christ.

Prayer: Lord, I want to act today in such a way that others may be happy to conclude that I am a Christian.

150 THE TRUE AND LIVING GOD

And when the crowds saw what Paul had done, they lifted up their voices, saying in Lycaonian, "The gods have come down to us in the likeness of men!" Barnabas they called Zeus, and Paul, because he was the chief speaker, they called Hermes. And the priest of Zeus, whose temple was in front of the city, brought oxen and garlands to the gates and wanted to offer sacrifice with the people. But when the apostles Barnabas and Paul heard of it, they tore their garments and rushed out among the multitude, crying, "Men, why are you doing this? We also are men, of like nature with you, and bring you good news, that you should turn from these vain things to a living God who made the heaven and the earth and the sea and all that is in them. In past generations he allowed all the nations to walk in their own ways; yet he did not leave himself without witness, for he did good and gave you from heaven rains and fruitful seasons, satisfying your hearts with food and gladness." (*Acts 14:11–17*)

Key Ideas: The Gospel of turning
A created universe
Our providential God

Action Step: Look closer on a familiar route you travel, seeking to be more aware of God's creative works in nature.

Prayer: Lord, I know You are expecting me, as a creative caretaker, to treat this earth today in a responsible manner.

151 THE JERUSALEM CONFERENCE

The apostles and the elders were gathered together to consider this matter. And after there had been much debate, Peter rose and said to them, "Brethren, you know that in the early days God made choice among you, that by my mouth the Gentiles should hear the word of the gospel and believe. And God who knows the heart bore witness to them, giving them the Holy Spirit just as he did to us; and he made no distinction between us and them, but cleansed their hearts by faith. Now therefore why do you make trial of God by putting a yoke upon the neck of the disciples which neither our fathers nor we have been able to bear? But we believe that we shall be saved through the grace of the Lord Jesus, just as they will." (*Acts 15:6–11*)

Key Ideas: The undeniable truth of experience
Drawing lines where God does not
We can't save ourselves

Action Step: Give new and different organizations and movements an opportunity to demonstrate whether or not they are the work of God's Spirit.

Prayer: Lord, help me not to restrict the freedom of others today out of selfish or fearful motives.

152 WHERE THERE IS A NEED

And they went through the region of Phrygia and Galatia, having been forbidden by the Holy Spirit to speak the word in Asia. And when they had come opposite Mysia, they attempted to go into Bithynia, but the Spirit of Jesus did not allow them; so, passing by Mysia, they went down to Troas. And a vision appeared to Paul in the night: a man of Macedonia was standing beseeching him and saying, "Come over to Macedonia and help us." And when he had seen the vision, immediately we sought to go on into Macedonia, concluding that God had called us to preach the gospel to them. (*Acts 16:6–10*)

Key Ideas: Promptings from the Spirit
A stranger in the night
Interpreting our visions

Action Step: Follow through on a recent inspiration by writing down a sequence of steps for its fulfillment.

Prayer: Lord, make me alert to the open door today, even if many others are closed.

153 SOUL-SHAKING EVENT

But about midnight Paul and Silas were praying and singing hymns to God, and the prisoners were listening to them, and suddenly there was a great earthquake, so that the foundations of the prison were shaken; and immediately all the doors were opened and every one's fetters were unfastened. When the jailer woke and saw that the prison doors were open, he drew his sword and was about to kill himself, supposing that the prisoners had escaped. But Paul cried with a loud voice, "Do not harm yourself, for we are all here." And he called for lights and rushed in, and trembling with fear he fell down before Paul and Silas, and brought them out and said, "Men, what must I do to be saved?" And they said, "Believe in the Lord Jesus, and you will be saved, you and your household." And they spoke the word of the Lord to him and to all that were in his house. And he took them the same hour of the night, and washed their wounds, and he was baptized at once, with all his family. (*Acts 16:25–33*)

Key Ideas: The awesome acts of God
Help for the gatekeepers
The Word and the washing

Action Step: Play on your instruments, sing, or whistle one of your favorite hymns even if you aren't in church.

Prayer: If the world around me is shaken today, Lord, give me a word of hope and cheer to speak to my fearful fellow human beings.

154 OPENNESS TO SCRIPTURE

But the Jews were jealous, and taking some wicked fellows of the rabble, they gathered a crowd, set the city in an uproar, and attacked the house of Jason, seeking to bring them out to the people. And when they could not find them, they dragged Jason and some of the brethren before the city authorities, crying, "These men who have turned the world upside down have come here also, and Jason has received them; and they are all acting against the decrees of Caesar, saying that there is another king, Jesus." And the people and the city authorities were disturbed when they heard this. And when they had taken security from Jason and the rest, they let them go. The brethren immediately sent Paul and Silas away by night to Beroea; and when they arrived they went into the Jewish synagogue. Now these Jews were more noble than those in Thessalonica, for they received the word with all eagerness, examining the scriptures daily to see if these things were so. (*Acts 17:5–11*)

Key Ideas: Generating spiritual earthquakes
The Christian presence: a political force
Daily Scripture study by the people

Action Step: Become acquainted with some of the contemporary commentaries and Bible study books that contain balanced Biblical scholarship and interpretation.

Prayer: Today, Lord, I will look at the Scripture with critical and open eyes and not with filtered lenses of prejudice.

155 FINDING GOD

"The God who made the world and everything in it, being Lord of heaven and earth, does not live in shrines made by man, nor is he served by human hands, as though he needed anything, since he himself gives to all men life and breath and everything. And he made from one every nation of men to live on all the face of the earth, having determined allotted periods and the boundaries of their habitation, that they should seek God, in the hope that they might feel after him and find him. Yet he is not far from each one of us, for

> In him we live and move and have our being;

as even some of your poets have said,

> For we are indeed his offspring.

Being then God's offspring, we ought not to think that the Deity is like gold, or silver, or stone, a representation by the art and imagination of man. The times of ignorance God overlooked, but now he commands all men everywhere to repent, because he has fixed a day on which he will judge the world in righteousness by a man whom he has appointed, and of this he has given assurance to all men by raising him from the dead." *(Acts 17:24–31)*

Key Ideas: Man-made gods
God who made man
God's special Man

Action Step: Try to explain to a child or adult in your own words your belief in God as Creator, who is omnipresent and who is revealed in Jesus.

Prayer: Lord, today I am going to look for You in every moment and every experience of my life and world.

156 DEEPENING FAITH'S UNDERSTANDING

Now a Jew named Apollos, a native of Alexandria, came to Ephesus. He was an eloquent man, well versed in the scriptures. He had been instructed in the way of the Lord; and being fervent in spirit, he spoke and taught accurately the things concerning Jesus, though he knew only the baptism of John. He began to speak boldly in the synagogue; but when

Priscilla and Aquila heard him, they took him and expounded to him the way of God more accurately. And when he wished to cross to Achaia, the brethren encouraged him, and wrote to the disciples to receive him. When he arrived, he greatly helped those who through grace had believed, for he powerfully confuted the Jews in public, showing by the scriptures that the Christ was Jesus. (*Acts 18:24–28*)

Key Ideas: Every ability in the service of Christ
A willingness to keep growing
Teaching even the talented

Action Step: Find a way to challenge a capable friend or fellow worker toward further usefulness in the Kingdom of God.

Prayer: Keep me growing today, Lord, as I expect others to grow.

157 MOTIVES FOR THE MINISTRY

"And now, behold, I am going to Jerusalem, bound in the Spirit, not knowing what shall befall me there; except that the Holy Spirit testifies to me in every city that imprisonment and afflictions await me. But I do not account my life of any value nor as precious to myself, if only I may accomplish my course and the ministry which I received from the Lord Jesus, to testify to the gospel of the grace of God. And now, behold, I know that all you among whom I have gone preaching the kingdom will see my face no more. Therefore I testify to you this day that I am innocent of the blood of all of you, for I did not shrink from declaring to you the whole counsel of God. Take heed to yourselves and to all the flock, in which the Holy Spirit has made you overseers to care for the church of God which he obtained for himself with the blood of His own. I know that after my departure fierce wolves will come in among you, not sparing the flock; and from among your own selves will arise men speaking perverse things, to draw away the disciples after them. Therefore be alert, remembering that for three years I did not cease night or day to admonish every one with tears. And now I commend you to God and to the word of his grace, which is able to build you up and to give you the inheritance among all those who are consecrated. I coveted no one's silver or gold or apparel. You yourselves know that these hands ministered to my necessities, and to those who were with me. In all things I have shown you that by so toiling one must help the weak, remembering the words of the Lord Jesus, how he said, 'It is more blessed to give than to receive.' " (*Acts 20:22–35*)

Key Ideas: The strong propulsion of the Trinity
The burden of the Word
The generosity of Jesus' ministers

Action Step: Get to know your minister personally; make it possible for him or her to get acquainted with you.

Prayer: Lord, today I resolve to become a friend to my minister, since I assume he or she wants to be my friend.

158 GOD'S TROUBLING LIGHTS

"I persecuted this Way to the death, binding and delivering to prison both men and women, as the high priest and the whole council of elders bear me witness. From them I received letters to the brethren, and I journeyed to Damascus to take those also who were there and bring them in bonds to Jerusalem to be punished. As I made my journey and drew near to Damascus, about noon a great light from heaven suddenly shone about me. And I fell to the ground and heard a voice saying to me, 'Saul, Saul, why do you persecute me?' And I answered, 'Who are you, Lord?' And he said to me, 'I am Jesus of Nazareth whom you are persecuting.' " (*Acts 22:4–8*)

Key Ideas: Sincerity can be blind
A journey into light
Jesus is the living Christ

Action Step: Be willing to encounter anyone who may have hard and critical questions about Christianity; some people are seriously searching in spite of their apparent antagonism.

Prayer: Lord, I want to live today in Your correcting and kindling light.

159 ON TRIAL FOR A HOPE

"My manner of life from my youth, spent from the beginning among my own nation and at Jerusalem, is known by all the Jews. They have known for a long time, if they are willing to testify, that according to the strictest party of our religion I have lived as a Pharisee. And now I stand here on trial for hope in the promise made by God to our fathers, to which our twelve tribes hope to attain, as they earnestly worship night and day. And for this hope I am accused by Jews, O king! Why is it thought incredible by any of you that God raises the dead?" (*Acts 26:4–8*)

Key Ideas: A tradition of faith
Following our hopes
The great confirmation of God's power

Action Step: Review your religious heritage in whatever way helpful—conversations with family, research, remembered experiences—treasure the best that has been handed on to you.

Prayer: Lord, if I have the opportunity today to prove that Your power in the ancient days is still real in our times, make me daring with faith.

160 THE HEAVENLY VISION

"And when we had all fallen to the ground, I heard a voice saying to me in the Hebrew language, 'Saul, Saul, why do you persecute me? It hurts you to kick against the goads.' And I said, 'Who are you, Lord?' And the Lord said, 'I am Jesus whom you are persecuting. But rise and stand upon your feet; for I have appeared to you for this purpose, to appoint you to serve and bear witness to the things in which you have seen me and to those in which I will appear to you, delivering you from the people and from the Gentiles—to whom I send you to open their eyes, that they may turn from darkness to light and from the power of Satan to God, that they may receive forgiveness of sins and a place among those who are consecrated by faith in me.' " (*Acts 26:14–18*)

Key Ideas: Encounter with the living Christ
Appointment to adventure
Conversion is for the whole world

Action Step: Make an inquiry of several long-time Christians and ask them, "What are the greatest blessings and rewards you have experienced in life with and service to Jesus Christ?"

Prayer: Lord, I am present today, listening to Your voice, reporting for duty.

161 THE GOSPEL

For I am not ashamed of the gospel: it is the power of God for salvation to every one who has faith, to the Jew first and also to the Greek. For in it the righteousness of God is revealed through faith for faith; as it is written, "He who through faith is righteous shall live." (*Romans 1:16, 17*)

Key Ideas: The super-charged story of Christ
Salvation is for everyone
Faith leads to life

Action Step: The next time Christianity or the Church is spoken about in one of your circles of association, talk without embarrassment about the benefits you have personally experienced as a Christian.

Prayer: Lord, I want to act enthusiastically today upon what I say I believe.

162 EVERYONE A SINNER

But now the righteousness of God has been manifested apart from law, although the law and the prophets bear witness to it, the righteousness of God through faith in Jesus Christ for all who believe. For there is no distinction; since all have sinned and fall short of the glory of God, they are justified by his grace as a gift, through the redemption which is in Christ Jesus, whom God put forward as an expiation by his blood, to be received by faith. (*Romans 3:21–25*)

Key Ideas: The right way of living—through faith
Rebellion against God is universal
The redemption God has given us

Action Step: Help someone to discover that the Church is for everyone, especially for admitted and repentant sinners.

Prayer: Today, Lord, I am not going to allow my awareness of inadequacies and sins to cloud out the sunshine of Your forgiving love.

163 THE FATHER OF FAITH

That is why it depends on faith, in order that the promise may rest on grace and be guaranteed to all his descendants—not only to the adherents of the law but also to those who share the faith of Abraham, for he is the father of us all, as it is written, "I have made you the father of many nations"—in the presence of the God in whom he believed, who gives life to the dead and calls into existence the things that do not exist. In hope he believed against hope, that he should become the father of many nations; as he had been told, "So shall your descendants be." He did not weaken in faith when he considered his own body, which was as good as dead because he was about a hundred years old, or when he considered the barrenness of Sarah's womb. No distrust made him waver concerning the promise of God, but he grew strong in his faith as he gave glory to God, fully convinced that God was able to do what he had promised. That is why his faith was "reckoned to him as righteousness." But the words, "it was reckoned to him," were written not for his sake alone, but for ours also. It will be reckoned to us who believe in him that raised from the dead Jesus our Lord, who was put to death for our trespasses and raised for our justification. (*Romans 4:16–25*)

Key Ideas: In the beginning was faith
What faith is like
The new test of faith

Action Step: Recall any efforts or accomplishments you have been involved in about which you or someone else said, "It can't be done." Have a good time rejoicing.

Prayer: Lord, I am learning slowly, but it is still difficult for me today to believe in Your great power to bring our "human impossibilities" into "divine actualities."

164 CALLED TO ENDURANCE

Therefore, since we are justified by faith, we have peace with God through our Lord Jesus Christ. Through him we have obtained access to this grace in which we stand, and we rejoice in our hope of sharing the glory of God. More than that, we rejoice in our sufferings, knowing that suffering produces endurance, and endurance produces character, and character produces hope, and hope does not disappoint us, because God's love has been poured into our hearts through the Holy Spirit which has been given to us. (*Romans 5:1–5*)

Key Ideas: Jesus opened up fellowship with God
Growth through trials
Why our hope is sure

Action Step: Turn a recent disappointment into an occasion to be more sensitive to someone who is facing a similar predicament.

Prayer: Only You, Lord, can open my eyes today to see the good in the things I am called to endure.

165 CHRIST FOR US

While we were yet weak at the right time Christ died for the ungodly. Why, one will hardly die for a righteous man—though perhaps for a good man one will dare even to die. But God shows his love for us in that while we were yet sinners Christ died for us. Since, therefore, we are now justified by his blood, much more shall we be saved by him from the wrath of God. For if while we were enemies we were reconciled to God by the death of his Son, much more, now that we are reconciled, shall we be saved by his life. (*Romans 5:6–10*)

Key Ideas: God's providence in spite of our sins
God's love in Jesus' dying
God's power in Jesus' rising

Action Step: Risk speaking the Good News—God is not our enemy but our Friend—to a troubled or confused friend.

Prayer: Lord, I will remember today what my life and world would be like if Jesus had not lived and died for me.

166 BAPTIZED WITH CHRIST

Do you not know that all of us who have been baptized into Christ Jesus were baptized into his death? We were buried therefore with him by baptism into death, so that as Christ was raised from the dead by the glory of the Father, we too might walk in newness of life. For if we have been united with him in a death like his, we shall certainly be united with him in a resurrection like his. We know that our old self was crucified with him so that the sinful body might be destroyed, and we might no longer be enslaved to sin. For he who has died is freed from sin. But if we have died with Christ, we believe that we shall also live with him. (*Romans 6:3–8*)

Key Ideas: A ceremony of new life
One with Jesus' death and resurrection
Sin can be dealt with

Action Step: Invite persons in your Christian fellowship to tell about Christ's power in changing their lives.

Prayer: I have been baptized into Christ and because of this, Lord, I know You are not going to let me forget today the consequences of that commitment.

167 NEW USEFULNESS

When you were slaves of sin, you were free in regard to righteousness. But then what return did you get from the things of which you are now ashamed? The end of those things is death. But now that you have been set free from sin and have become slaves of God, the return you get is sanctification and its end, eternal life. For the wages of sin is death, but the free gift of God is eternal life in Christ Jesus our Lord. (*Romans 6:20–23*)

Key Ideas: Slaves of sin
Slaves of God
Satisfactions of salvation

Action Step: Examine your recent decisions about money, free time, and things that are urgent or essential to you; are you motivated to serve God or yourself?

Prayer: Today, I want very much, Lord, to experience the holy and obedient way of Christ that can endure beyond the corrosions of human time.

168 THE WAR WITHIN

So I find it to be a law that when I want to do right, evil lies close at hand. For I delight in the law of God, in my inmost self, but I see in my members another law at war with the law of my mind and making me captive to the law of sin which dwells in my members. Wretched man that I am! Who will deliver me from this body of death? Thanks be to God through Jesus Christ our Lord! (*Romans 7:21–25*)

Key Ideas: The pull toward evil
The inspiration of God's Law
The great deliverance

Action Step: Do one good thing this day that is difficult or that you don't especially want to do.

Prayer: Lord, about the time I think I have put it all together I do something less than my best, and therefore I need Your help today to keep on toward the better way.

169 THE SPIRIT OF LIFE

There is therefore now no condemnation for those who are in Christ Jesus. For the law of the Spirit of life in Christ Jesus has set me free from the law of sin and death. For God has done what the law, weakened by the flesh, could not do: sending his own Son in the likeness of sinful flesh and for sin, he condemned sin in the flesh, in order that the just requirement of the law might be fulfilled in us, who walk not according to the flesh but according to the Spirit. For those who live according to the flesh set their minds on the things of the flesh, but those who live according to the Spirit set their minds on the things of the Spirit. To set the mind on the flesh is death, but to set the mind on the Spirit is life and peace. (*Romans 8:1–6*)

Key Ideas: Release from full punishment
God's special rescue mission
Revaluing our directions

Action Step: Choose one of the enlivening and enduring qualities of a Spirit-directed life and try to expand its application in your own life.

Prayer: Lord, because of your mercy there is a different force working within me now, one that I want to show to everyone I meet today.

170 THE SPIRIT OF CHRIST

But you are not in the flesh, you are in the Spirit, if in fact the Spirit of God dwells in you. Any one who does not have the Spirit of Christ does not belong to him. But if Christ is in you, although your bodies are dead because of sin, your spirits are alive because of righteousness. If the Spirit of him who raised Jesus from the dead dwells in you, he who raised Christ Jesus from the dead will give life to your mortal bodies also through his Spirit which dwells in you. (*Romans 8:9–11*)

Key Ideas: The true test of a Christian
A goodness that God gives us
Participation in Christ's resurrection

Action Step: Decide to permit no barrier to prevent friendship between yourself and other Christians in whom the Spirit of Christ is present.

Prayer: Lord, You are today the very life of this frail human frame of mine.

171 LED BY THE SPIRIT

So then, brethren, we are debtors, not to the flesh, to live according to the flesh—for if you live according to the flesh you will die, but if by the Spirit you put to death the deeds of the body you will live. For all who are led by the Spirit of God are sons of God. For you did not receive the spirit of slavery to fall back into fear, but you have received the spirit of sonship. When we cry, "Abba! Father!" it is the Spirit himself bearing witness with our spirit that we are children of God, and if children, then heirs, heirs of God and fellow heirs with Christ, provided we suffer with him in order that we may also be glorified with him. I consider that the sufferings of this present time are not worth comparing with the glory that is to be revealed to us. (*Romans 8:12–18*)

Key Ideas: The empowering Spirit
The liberating Spirit
The promising Spirit

Action Step: Be especially alert in this day's activities to the ways God's holy presence is trying to work through you and your relationships with people.

Prayer: Lord, today it is enough for me to say, "I love You."

172 CREATION CONTINUES

For the creation waits with eager longing for the revealing of the sons of God; for the creation was subjected to futility, not of its own will but by the will of him who subjected it in hope; because the creation itself will be set free from its bondage to decay and obtain the glorious liberty of the children of God. We know that the whole creation has been groaning in travail together until now; and not only the creation, but we ourselves, who have the first fruits of the Spirit, groan inwardly as we wait for adoption as sons, the redemption of our bodies. For in this hope we were saved. Now hope that is seen is not hope. For who hopes for what he sees?

But if we hope for what we do not see, we wait for it with patience. Likewise the Spirit helps us in our weakness; for we do not know how to pray as we ought, but the Spirit himself intercedes for us with sighs too deep for words. And he who searches the hearts of men knows what is the mind of the Spirit, because the Spirit intercedes for the saints according to the will of God. (*Romans 8:19–27*)

Key Ideas: The incompleteness of creation
The final deliverance of creation
The healing attitude of hope

Action Step: Support the scientific rethinking about the factors that will be necessary to control and utilize technology for our human as well as material progress.

Prayer: Lord, make me alert and rigorous in my thinking today in order that I may participate intelligently in the development of a better quality of life spiritually and materially for the human race.

173 THE UNDEFEATABLE LIFE

We know that in everything God works for good with those who love him, who are called according to his purpose. For those whom he foreknew he also predestined to be conformed to the image of his Son, in order that he might be the first-born among many brethren. And those whom he predestined he also called; and those whom he called he also justified; and those whom he justified he also glorified. What then shall we say to this? If God is for us, who is against us? He who did not spare his own Son but gave him up for us all, will he not also give us all things with him? Who shall bring any charge against God's elect? It is God who justifies; who is to condemn? Is it Christ Jesus, who died, yes, who was raised from the dead, who is at the right hand of God, who indeed intercedes for us? Who shall separate us from the love of Christ? Shall tribulation, or distress, or persecution, or famine, or nakedness, or peril, or sword? As it is written,

> For thy sake we are being killed all the day long; we are regarded as sheep to be slaughtered.

No, in all these things we are more than conquerors through him who loved us. For I am sure that neither death, nor life, nor angels, nor principalities, nor things present, nor things to come, nor powers, nor height, nor depth, nor anything else in all creation, will be able to separate us from the love of God in Christ Jesus our Lord. (*Romans 8:28–39*)

Key Ideas: God's purpose for our good
God's gifts to us through Christ
God's love never lets up

Action Step: Deliver your personal word of hope about God's persistent love in tough times to someone in sorrow or suffering.

Prayer: Lord, I will hold firm in my faith in You today because I know You will hold me even through my doubts, depressions, and defeats.

174 RELIGIOUS ROOTS

For I could wish that I myself were accursed and cut off from Christ for the sake of my brethren, my kinsmen by race. They are Israelites, and to them belong the sonship, the glory, the covenants, the giving of the law, the worship, and the promises; to them belong the patriarchs, and of their race, according to the flesh, is the Christ. God who is over all be blessed forever. Amen. But it is not as though the word of God had failed. For not all who are descended from Israel belong to Israel, and not all are children of Abraham because they are his descendants; but, "Your descendants will be reckoned through Isaac." This means that it is not the children of the flesh who are the children of God, but the children of the promise are reckoned as descendants. (*Romans 9:3–8*)

Key Ideas: The natural love of our own race
The great heritage of Israel
Descendants of the faith

Action Step: Acquire a calendar listing of the Jewish high holy days, and learn about the basic religious beliefs of contemporary Jews.

Prayer: Lord, I truly wish to personally demonstrate the Christ life today, so that all may see and believe that Jesus is the Messiah.

175 INTERNALIZING THE WORD

Moses writes that the man who practices the righteousness which is based on the law shall live by it. But the righteousness based on faith says, "Do not say in your heart, 'Who will ascend into heaven?' (that is, to bring Christ down) or 'Who will descend into the abyss?' " (that is, to bring Christ up from the dead). But what does it say? "The word is near you, on your lips and in your heart" (that is, the word of faith which we preach); because, if you confess with your lips that Jesus is Lord and believe in your heart that God raised him from the dead, you will be saved. For man believes with his heart and so is justified, and he confesses with his lips and so is saved. The scripture says, "No one who believes in him will be put to shame." For there is no distinction between Jew and Greek; the same Lord is Lord of all and bestows his riches upon all who call upon him. For, "every one who calls upon the name of the Lord will be saved." (*Romans 10:5–13*)

Key Ideas: The inward faith of Israel
The inward faith of the Church
The inclusive invitation of Christ

Action Step: In writing and in the plainest language possible, tell how you would describe to a non-Christian what it means to have Jesus Christ living in your heart.

Prayer: Lord, I will try to live by as much of Your Word as I know today.

176 THE IMPORTANCE OF PREACHING

But how are men to call upon him in whom they have not believed? And how are they to believe in him of whom they have never heard? And how are they to hear without a preacher? And how can men preach unless they are sent? As it is written, "How beautiful are the feet of those who preach good news!" But they have not all obeyed the gospel; for Isaiah says, "Lord, who has believed what he has heard from us?" So faith comes from what is heard, and what is heard comes by the preaching of Christ. (*Romans 10:14–17*)

Key Ideas: Belief is the basis of salvation
A special mission for preachers
All Christian preaching is dialogue

Action Step: Encourage scholarship assistance or support of one of your church's ministerial educational centers (college, seminary, or continuing education center).

Prayer: Thank You, Lord, for those interpreters of Your Good News who are bringing the faith to us today.

177 NO SUBSTITUTE SACRIFICES

I appeal to you therefore, brethren, by the mercies of God, to present your bodies as a living sacrifice, holy and acceptable to God, which is your spiritual worship. Do not be conformed to this world but be transformed by the renewal of your mind, that you may prove what is the will of God, what is good and acceptable and perfect. For by the grace given to me I bid every one among you not to think of himself more highly than he ought to think, but to think with sober judgment, each according to the measure of faith which God has assigned him. For as in one body we have many members, and all the members do not have the same function, so we, though many, are one body in Christ, and individually members one of another. Having gifts that differ according to the grace given to us, let us use them: if prophecy, in proportion to our faith; if service, in our serving; he who teaches, in his teaching; he who exhorts, in his exhortation; he who contributes, in liberality; he who gives aid, with zeal; he who does acts of mercy, with cheerfulness. (*Romans 12:1–8*)

Key Ideas: Commitment that is complete
Conformity to Christ or culture?
Conversion continues

Action Step: Keep the worship service of God going beyond the church sanctuary (in the fields, factory, office, school, and home).

Prayer: Today, Lord, I will try to keep my fellowship with You as my primary commitment compared with all other commitments.

178 LIVING TOGETHER

Let love be genuine; hate what is evil, hold fast to what is good; love one another with brotherly affection; outdo one another in showing honor. Never flag in zeal, be aglow with the Spirit, serve the Lord. Rejoice in your hope, be patient in tribulation, be constant in prayer. Contribute to the needs of the saints, practice hospitality. Bless those who persecute you; bless and do not curse them. Rejoice with those who rejoice, weep with those who weep. Live in harmony with one another; do not be haughty, but associate with the lowly; never be conceited. Repay no one evil for evil, but take thought for what is noble in the sight of all. If possible, so far as it depends upon you, live peaceably with all. Beloved, never avenge yourselves, but leave it to the wrath of God; for it is written, "Vengeance is mine, I will repay, says the Lord." No, "if your enemy is hungry, feed him; if he is thirsty, give him drink; for by so doing you will heap burning coals upon his head." Do not be overcome by evil, but overcome evil with good. (*Romans 12:9–21*)

Key Ideas: Positive personalities for Christ
Encouragement for endurance
The wisdom of nonretaliation

Action Step: Prepare or follow through with aggressive goodwill on some personal help project even if you must become vulnerable to do so.

Prayer: I am turning over to You, today, Lord, my resentments and hates, since they are more than I can afford to carry another day.

179 GOOD CITIZENS

Let every person be subject to the governing authorities. For there is no authority except from God, and those that exist have been instituted by God. Therefore he who resists the authorities resists what God has appointed, and those who resist will incur judgment. For rulers are not a terror to good conduct, but to bad. Would you have no fear of him who is in authority? Then do what is good, and you will receive his approval, for he is God's servant for your good. But if you do wrong, be afraid, for he does not bear the sword in vain; he is the servant of God to execute his wrath on the wrong-doer. Therefore one must be subject, not only to avoid God's wrath but also for the sake of conscience. For the same reason you also pay taxes, for the authorities are ministers of God, attending to this very thing. Pay all of them their dues, taxes to whom taxes are due, revenue to whom revenue is due, respect to whom respect is due, honor to whom honor is due. Owe no one anything, except to love one another; for he who loves his neighbor has fulfilled the law. (*Romans 13:1–8*)

Key Ideas: Good governments from God
The necessity of laws
Paying our dues to society

Action Step: As an informed citizen vote for and support only those government policies that are based on honesty, justice, and respect for persons and that will enhance the general good of all.

Prayer: I will be an active and respectable citizen today, Lord, regardless of the cost.

180 LIVING IN THE LIGHT

For salvation is nearer to us now than when we first believed; the night is far gone, the day is at hand. Let us then cast off the works of darkness and put on the armor of light; let us conduct ourselves becomingly as in the day, not in reveling and drunkenness, not in debauchery and licentiousness, not in quarreling and jealousy. But put on the Lord Jesus Christ, and make no provision for the flesh, to gratify its desires. (*Romans 13:11–14*)

Key Ideas: Christians on alert
Discarding the ways of darkness
A Christian's dress code

Action Step: Promote some good participation recreation alternatives in your neighborhood or community.

Prayer: Trouble my conscience today, Lord, if I dabble in morally questionable activities.

181 CHRISTIAN LIBERTY

One man esteems one day as better than another, while another man esteems all days alike. Let every one be fully convinced in his own mind. He who observes the day, observes it in honor of the Lord. He also who eats, eats in honor of the Lord, since he gives thanks to God; while he who abstains, abstains in honor of the Lord and gives thanks to God. None of us lives to himself, and none of us dies to himself. If we live, we live to the Lord, and if we die, we die to the Lord; so then, whether we live or whether we die, we are the Lord's. For to this end Christ died and lived again, that he might be Lord both of the dead and of the living. (*Romans 14:5–9*)

Key Ideas: Liberty under one Lord
Life together with one Lord
Love embodied by one Lord

Action Step: Courageously encounter expressions of coercion that seek to force every Christian into conformity with a uniform mold or style.

Prayer: Lord, I will give the persons I meet today space to follow You in their own unique style.

Then let us no more pass judgment on one another, but rather decide never to put a stumbling block or hindrance in the way of a brother. I know and am persuaded in the Lord Jesus that nothing is unclean in itself; but it is unclean for any one who thinks it unclean. If your brother is being injured by what you eat, you are no longer walking in love. Do not let what you eat cause the ruin of one for whom Christ died. So do not let your good be spoken of as evil. For the kingdom of God is not food and drink but righteousness and peace and joy in the Holy Spirit; he who thus serves Christ is acceptable to God and approved by men. Let us then pursue what makes for peace and for mutual upbuilding. Do not, for the sake of food, destroy the work of God. (*Romans 14:13–20*)

Key Ideas: God's good creation
Bound together because of Christ
The Kingdom of peace and growth

Action Step: Discard a questionable habit that may be misleading others while still staying a free person yourself.

Prayer: Lord, make me a blessing instead of a barrier to my brothers and sisters today.

183 HARMONY IN HELPING OTHERS

We who are strong ought to bear with the failings of the weak, and not to please ourselves; let each of us please his neighbor for his good, to edify him. For Christ did not please himself; but, as it is written, "The reproaches of those who reproached thee fell on me." For whatever was written in former days was written for our instruction, that by steadfastness and by the encouragement of the scriptures we might have hope. May the God of steadfastness and encouragement grant you to live in such harmony with one another, in accord with Christ Jesus, that together you may with one voice glorify the God and Father of Our Lord Jesus Christ. (*Romans 15:1–6*)

Key Ideas: Christ cared for the weak
Inspiration in ancient Scriptures
One in faith and witness

Action Step: Cultivate Christian friendships with persons of common causes in your community.

Prayer: Today, Lord, let me point toward You instead of my own group in a sectarian way.

184 THE WISDOM AND THE POWER

For the word of the cross is folly to those who are perishing, but to us who are being saved it is the power of God. For it is written,

> I will destroy the wisdom of the wise, and the cleverness of the clever I will thwart.

Where is the wise man? Where is the scribe? Where is the debater of this age? Has not God made foolish the wisdom of the world? For since, in the wisdom of God, the world did not know God through wisdom, it pleased God through the folly of what we preach to save those who believe. For Jews demand signs and Greeks seek wisdom, but we preach Christ crucified, a stumbling block to Jews and folly to Gentiles, but to those who are called, both Jews and Greeks, Christ the power of God and the wisdom of God. For the foolishness of God is wiser than men, and the weakness of God is stronger than men. (*I Corinthians 1:18–25*)

Key Ideas: The Cross is the power of God
The wisdom of God we preach
God is greater than our limitations

Action Step: Encourage the authentic preaching of Christ—the reality of God's love through Christ's suffering—and discourage the preaching of cheap grace or clever controversy.

Prayer: Lord, it is for me a deep consolation today to know that my salvation does not rest in my own power or shrewdness, but in You.

185 HUMBLE BEGINNINGS

For consider your call, brethren; not many of you were wise according to worldly standards, not many were powerful, not many were of noble birth; but God chose what is foolish in the world to shame the wise, God chose what is weak in the world to shame the strong, God chose what is low and despised in the world, even things that are not, to bring to nothing things that are, so that no human being might boast in the presence of God. He is the source of your life in Christ Jesus, whom God made our wisdom, our righteousness and consecration and redemption;

therefore, as it is written, "Let him who boasts, boast of the Lord." *(I Corinthians 1:26–31)*

Key Ideas: God's call to become
God's gift of the Christ
The glory belongs to God

Action Step: Make sure the church you attend and work in welcomes without prejudice persons of every social class in your community.

Prayer: Lord, who am I to say that only a certain group of people can belong to Your Church?

186 PREACHING CHRIST CRUCIFIED

For I decided to know nothing among you except Jesus Christ and him crucified. And I was with you in weakness and in much fear and trembling; and my speech and my message were not in plausible words of wisdom, but in demonstration of the Spirit and of power, that your faith might not rest in the wisdom of men but in the power of God. *(I Corinthians 2:2–5)*

Key Ideas: The central message of preaching
The unique manner of preaching
The goal of Christian preaching

Action Step: Make a request of your minister that he or she preach a sermon on a subject that may answer one of your deepest questions about Jesus, the Christ.

Prayer: I remember my minister today, and ask that he or she be guided not only with insights in interpretation but also with Your empowering love.

187 THE SECRET DISCLOSED

Yet among the mature we do impart wisdom, although it is not a wisdom of this age or of the rulers of this age, who are doomed to pass away. But we impart a secret and hidden wisdom of God, which God decreed before the ages for our glorification. None of the rulers of this age understood this; for if they had, they would not have crucified the Lord of glory. But, as it is written,

What no eye has seen, nor ear heard, nor the heart of man conceived, what God has prepared for those who love him,

God has revealed to us through the Spirit. *(I Corinthians 2:6–10)*

Key Ideas: God's plan now fulfilled
The undreamed-of came true
Sensitized by the Spirit

Action Step: In the evening spend some time out under the stars looking up and asking the God of our universe what He is saying to you personally as well as to the whole human race.

Prayer: I thank You, Lord, that Your promises are not all just for tomorrow but have been made real for us today in Jesus Christ.

188 FELLOW WORKERS

What then is Apollos? What is Paul? Servants through whom you believed, as the Lord assigned to each. I planted, Apollos watered, but God gave the growth. So neither he who plants nor he who waters is anything, but only God who gives the growth. He who plants and he who waters are equal, and each shall receive his wages according to his labor. For we are God's fellow workers; you are God's field, God's building. *(I Corinthians 3:5–9)*

Key Ideas: Great personalities are gifts from God
God is the ground of our growth
God is working in our working together

Action Step: Make a time chart for your Christian fellowship or parish listing many of the saints and Christian leaders of the Church up through the centuries.

Prayer: Lord, give me today the right perspective in history of the long flow of spiritual leaders who have contributed resources to the present Church.

189 EVERYONE A BUILDER

According to the grace of God given to me, like a skilled master builder I laid a foundation, and another man is building upon it. Let each man take care how he builds upon it. For no other foundation can any one lay than that which is laid, which is Jesus Christ. Now if any one builds on the foundation with gold, silver, precious stones, wood, hay, straw—each man's work will become manifest; for the Day will disclose it, because it will be revealed with fire, and the fire will test what sort of work each one has done. If the work which any man has built on the foundation survives, he will receive a reward. (*I Corinthians 3:10–14*)

Key Ideas: The solid foundation of Christ
Quality in Christian building
The test of excellence and endurance

Action Step: Take up your work with a new awareness of the choice before you: good quality or mediocre performance, product, or service.

Prayer: Today, Lord, I am not going to be satisfied with sloppy work even if others around me are settling for second best.

190 KEEPING THE CHURCH TRUE

Do you not know that a little leaven ferments the whole lump of dough? Cleanse out the old leaven that you may be fresh dough, as you really are unleavened. For Christ, our paschal lamb, has been sacrificed. Let us, therefore, celebrate the festival, not with the old leaven, the leaven of malice and evil, but with the unleavened bread of sincerity and truth. (*I Corinthians 5:6–8*)

Key Ideas: Become what you are
Christ: The end and beginning event
The covenant celebrated in life

Action Step: Quit blaming everything in the Church on everybody else; begin straightening it out by cleaning up your own life first.

Prayer: Lord, today I am ready to move forward with new hope in Your pilgrim people—the Church.

191 TEMPLES OF GOD

Do you not know that your bodies are members of Christ? Shall I therefore take the members of Christ and make them members of a prostitute? Never! Do you not know that he who joins himself to a prostitute becomes one body with her? For, as it is written, "The two shall become one flesh." But he who is united to the Lord becomes one Spirit with him. Shun immorality. Every other sin which a man commits is outside the body; but the immoral man sins against his own body. Do you not know that your body is a temple of the Holy Spirit within you, which you have from God? You are not your own; you were bought with a price. So glorify God in your body. (*I Corinthians 6:15–20*)

Key Ideas: Our bodies are members of Christ
The sin of sexual immorality
Our bodies belong to God

Action Step: Make opportunities to teach children and youth the sanctity of the body and the place of personhood in genuine human fulfillment.

Prayer: Lead me, Lord, to glorify You in all my ways today.

192 LOVE BUILDS UP

"Knowledge" puffs up, but love builds up. If any one imagines that he knows something, he does not yet know as he ought to know. But if one loves God, one is known by him. Hence, as to the eating of food offered to idols, we know that "an idol has no real existence," and that "there is no God but one." For although there may be so-called gods in heaven or on earth—as indeed there are many "gods" and many "lords"—yet for us there is one God, the Father, from whom are all things and for whom we exist, and one Lord, Jesus Christ, through whom are all things and through whom we exist. (*I Corinthians 8:1–6*)

Key Ideas: Knowledge tempered by love
Always contending gods
Our God over all

Action Step: Assume the responsibility of being a big brother or sister in the faith to a youth or beginning follower of Christ.

Prayer: Give me wisdom and patience today, Lord, in relating to all brothers and sisters, as I remember my own struggle for freedom in Christ.

193 ALL THINGS TO ALL PEOPLE

For though I am free from all men, I have made myself a slave to all, that I might win the more. To the Jews I became as a Jew, in order to win Jews; to those under the law I became as one under the law—though not being myself under the law—that I might win those under the law. To those outside the law I became as one outside the law—not being without law toward God but under the law of Christ—that I might win those outside the law. To the weak I become weak, that I might win the weak. I have become all things to all men, that I might by all means save some. I do it all for the sake of the gospel, that I may share in its blessings. Do you not know that in a race all the runners compete, but only one receives the prize? So run that you may obtain it. Every athlete exercises self-control in all things. They do it to receive a perishable wreath, but we an imperishable. Well, I do not run aimlessly, I do not box as one beating the air; but I pommel my body and subdue it, lest after preaching to others I myself should be disqualified. (*I Corinthians 9:19–27*)

Key Ideas: The principle of identification
A passion for sharing the Gospel
Preaching demands a disciplined self

Action Step: Welcome to your church a missionary or fraternal worker who has returned from overseas; ask how he or she has identified with the culture and concerns of the people with whom he or she is seeking to share the Christian faith.

Prayer: Sharpen my talents today, Lord, for strategic witnessing to the adventurous and daring life with Jesus my supreme Leader and Friend.

194 STRENGTH FROM GOD

Therefore let any one who thinks that he stands take heed lest he fall. No temptation has overtaken you that is not common to man. God is faithful, and he will not let you be tempted beyond your strength, but with the temptation will also provide the way of escape, that you may be able to endure it. (*I Corinthians 10:12, 13*)

Key Ideas: On guard against carelessness
We're in the boat together
We can count on God

Action Step: Cultivate some positive habits and healthy activities in areas of your life where temptations arise.

Prayer: Lord, steer my life straight today, because the subtlety and power of evil are too much for me alone.

195 CHRISTIAN TABLE FELLOWSHIP

The cup of blessing which we bless, is it not a participation in the blood of Christ? The bread which we break, is it not a participation in the body of Christ? Because there is one bread, we who are many are one body, for we all partake of the same bread. Consider the people of Israel, are not those who eat the sacrifices partners in the altar? What do I imply then? That food offered to idols is anything, or that an idol is anything? No, I imply that what pagans sacrifice they offer to demons and not to God. I do not want you to be partners with demons. You cannot drink the cup of the Lord and the cup of demons. You cannot partake of the table of the Lord and the table of demons. (*I Corinthians 10:16–21*)

Key Ideas: The cup of the great thanksgiving
We too are the broken bread
United at one table of the Lord

Action Step: Prepare yourself for participation at the Lord's table by self-evaluation; confession of sins; rehearsal of the life, death, and resurrection of Jesus our Christ; and expectation of His presence.

Prayer: Lord, grant me today a vision of the Lord's table as inclusive as the brotherly spirit of Jesus and exclusive only of those who cannot see Your love in Him.

196 IN REMEMBRANCE OF ME

For I received from the Lord what I also delivered to you, that the Lord Jesus on the night when he was betrayed took bread, and when he had given thanks, he broke it, and said, "This is my body which is broken for you. Do this in remembrance of me." In the same way also the cup, after supper, saying, "This cup is the new covenant in my blood. Do this, as often as you drink it, in remembrance of me." For as often as you eat this bread and drink the cup, you proclaim the Lord's death until he comes. Whoever, therefore, eats the bread or drinks the cup of the Lord in an unworthy manner will be guilty of profaning the body and blood of the Lord. Let a man examine himself, and so eat of the bread and drink of the cup. For any one who eats and drinks without discerning the body eats and drinks judgment upon himself. (*I Corinthians 11:23–29*)

Key Ideas: Ritual of covenant renewal
Sermon in sacrament
An invitation to each believer

Action Step: As a Christian commit yourself to share in the celebration of the Lord's Supper regularly and whenever offered by the church.

Prayer: Lord, today it is a great relief to know that I do not have to be worthy to commune with You, only that I must always keep the sacrament of the Supper with respect to the Body of Christ.

197 GIFTS OF THE SPIRIT

Now there are varieties of gifts, but the same Spirit; and there are varieties of service, but the same Lord; and there are varieties of working, but it is the same God who inspires them all in every one. To each is given the manifestation of the Spirit for the common good. To one is given through the Spirit the utterance of wisdom, and to another the utterance of knowledge according to the same Spirit, to another faith by the same Spirit, to another gifts of healing by the one Spirit, to another the working of miracles, to another prophecy, to another the ability to distinguish between spirits, to another various kinds of tongues, to another the interpretation of tongues. All these are inspired by one and the same Spirit, who apportions to each one individually as he wills. (*I Corinthians 12:4–11*)

Key Ideas: The many-splendored ministry of Christians
The goal of the common good
Our common spiritual resource

Action Step: Express in some celebrative symbols or recognitions the Church's conviction that each person has something to contribute to the life of the community.

Prayer: I will not stereotype the activity of Your Spirit today, Lord, but will make room for all that is true to Jesus the Christ.

198 THE BODY OF CHRIST

For just as the body is one and has many members, and all the members of the body, though many, are one body, so it is with Christ. For by one Spirit we were all baptized into one body—Jews or Greeks, slaves or free—and all were made to drink of one Spirit. For the body does not consist of one member but of many. If the foot should say, "Because I am not a hand, I do not belong to the body," that would not make it any less a part of the body. And if the ear should say, "Because I am not an eye, I do not belong to the body," that would not make it any less a part of the body. If the whole body were an eye, where would be the hearing? If the whole body were an ear, where would be the sense of smell? But as it is, God arranged the organs in the body, each one of them, as he chose. *(I Corinthians 12:12–18)*

Key Ideas: The Spirit life of the body of Christ
Our interdependent life
A place for everyone

Action Step: Offer to help a neighbor or friend by letting them know you need their help too.

Prayer: Lord, You alone can correct whatever "I" problem I face today that may be distorting my vision of myself and others.

199 UNSELFISH LOVE

If I speak in the tongues of men and of angels, but have not love, I am a noisy gong or a clanging cymbal. And if I have prophetic powers, and understand all mysteries and all knowledge, and if I have all faith, so as to remove mountains, but have not love, I am nothing. If I give away all I have, and if I deliver my body to be burned, but have not love, I gain nothing. Love is patient and kind; love is not jealous or boastful; it is not arrogant or rude. Love does not insist on its own way; it is not irritable or resentful; it does not rejoice at wrong, but rejoices in the right. Love bears all things, believes all things, hopes all things, endures all things. Love never ends; as for prophecy, it will pass away; as for tongues, they will cease; as for knowledge, it will pass away. For our knowledge is imperfect and our prophecy is imperfect; but when the perfect comes, the imperfect will pass away. When I was a child, I spoke like a child, I thought like a child, I reasoned like a child; when I became a man, I gave up childish ways. For now we see in a mirror dimly, but then face to face. Now I know in part; then I shall understand fully, even as I have been fully understood. So faith, hope, love abide, these three; but the greatest of these is love. (*I Corinthians 13:1–13*)

Key Ideas: Love without hypocrisy
Love with Christlike qualities
Love with a capacity for growth

Action Step: Make a copy of this chapter and begin memorizing it by reading it over once each day until you know it.

Prayer: The way of love is the way of excellence, and the high goal of my life today, Lord, because you have gone before me to show the way.

200 BUILDING UP THE CHURCH

If even lifeless instruments, such as the flute or the harp, do not give distinct notes, how will anyone know what is played? And if the bugle gives an indistinct sound, who will get ready for battle? So with yourselves; if you in a tongue utter speech that is not intelligible, how will anyone know what is said? For you will be speaking into the air. There are doubtless many different languages in the world, and none is without meaning; but if I do not know the meaning of the language, I shall be a foreigner to the speaker and the speaker a foreigner to me. So with yourselves; since you are eager for manifestations of the Spirit, strive to excel in building up the church. Therefore, he who speaks in a tongue should pray for the power to interpret. For if I pray in a tongue, my spirit prays but my mind is unfruitful. What am I to do? I will pray with the spirit and I will pray with the mind also; I will sing with the spirit and I will sing with the mind also. (*I Corinthians 14:7–15*)

Key Ideas: Caution against confusion
Clarity of worship speech
Constructive ways of the Christian

Action Step: Listen more carefully to yourself and to others within your Christian associations to hear whether your vocabulary effectively conveys your Christian faith and your feelings of faith.

Prayer: Lord, today in all that I say I am going to clarify rather than complicate the Good News I present about Christ and the Church.

201 SHARING, LISTENING, LEARNING

What then, brethren? When you come together, each one has a hymn, a lesson, a revelation, a tongue, or an interpretation. Let all things be done for edification. If any speak in a tongue, let there be only two or at most three, and each in turn; and let one interpret. But if there is no one to interpret, let each of them keep silence in church and speak to himself and to God. Let two or three prophets speak, and let the others weigh what is said. If a revelation is made to another sitting by, let the first be silent. For you can all prophesy one by one, so that all may learn and all be encouraged; and the spirits of prophets are subject to prophets. For God is not a God of confusion but of peace. (*I Corinthians 14:26–33*)

Key Ideas: Enabling worship
Respecting one another in church
Order within freedom

Action Step: Study the practice of your church and others; seek to understand reasons for form and opportunities for freedom within the worship celebration.

Prayer: Lord, I want to participate personally today in worship but not in a way selfishly insensitive to the needs and interests of others.

202 CHRIST, THE FIRST FRUITS

If Christ has not been raised, your faith is futile and you are still in your sins. Then those also who have fallen asleep in Christ have perished. If for this life only we have hoped in Christ, we are of all men most to be pitied. But in fact Christ has been raised from the dead, the first fruits of those who have fallen asleep. For as by a man came death, by a man has come also the resurrection of the dead. For as in Adam all die, so also in Christ shall all be made alive. But each in his own order: Christ the first fruits, then at his coming those who belong to Christ. Then comes the end, when he delivers the kingdom to God the Father after destroying every rule and every authority and power. For he must reign until he has put all his enemies under his feet. The last enemy to be destroyed is death. *(I Corinthians 15:17–26)*

Key Ideas: Life without Christ is hopeless
Christ was raised for us all
Death is finally defeated

Action Step: Evaluate the illusions of physical immortality expressed by our contemporary culture; consider how such illusions are being confronted by the Church.

Prayer: Today, Lord, in spite of the dark clouds hanging over my world, I know the clear day of Your great love will finally shine where and when You will it.

203 VICTORY OVER DEATH

The first man was from the earth, a man of dust; the second man is from heaven. As was the man of dust, so are those who are of the dust; and as is the man of heaven, so are those who are of heaven. Just as we have borne the image of the man of dust, we shall also bear the image of the man of heaven. I tell you this, brethren: flesh and blood cannot inherit the kingdom of God, nor does the perishable inherit the imperishable. Lo! I tell you a mystery. We shall not all sleep, but we shall all be changed, in a moment, in the twinkling of an eye, at the last trumpet. For the trumpet will sound, and the dead will be raised imperishable, and we shall be changed. For this perishable nature must put on the imperishable, and this mortal nature must put on immortality. When the perishable puts on the imperishable, and the mortal puts on immortality, then shall come to pass the saying that is written:

> Death is swallowed up in victory.
> O death, where is thy victory?
> O death, where is thy sting?

The sting of death is sin, and the power of sin is the law. But thanks be to God, who gives us the victory through our Lord Jesus Christ. Therefore, my beloved brethren, be steadfast, immovable, always abounding in the work of the Lord, knowing that in the Lord your labor is not in vain. (*I Corinthians 15:47–58*)

Key Ideas: Our final destiny with Christ
The great transformation
Laboring with the living Christ

Action Step: The next time you make a bereavement visit or go to a memorial service, express to the family your Christian conviction in the resurrection of the dead.

Prayer: Lord, today with this triumphant resurrection hope I feel a confidence within that steadies and sustains my soul.

204 SYSTEMATIC STEWARDSHIP

On the first day of every week, each of you is to put something aside and save, as he may prosper, so that contributions need not be made when I come. And when I arrive, I will send those whom you accredit by letter to carry your gift to Jerusalem. (*I Corinthians 16:2, 3*)

Key Ideas: Compassion for the needy
Consistency of contributions
Cooperative Christian mission

Action Step: Plan a personal or group visit to (or communicate with) one of your church's home missions or cooperative overseas projects.

Prayer: While others only talk and others shut their eyes, I am going to do something today, Lord, that shows I care about this hungering world.

205 CIRCLE OF CHRISTIAN COMFORT

Blessed be the God and Father of our Lord Jesus Christ, the Father of mercies and God of all comfort, who comforts us in all our affliction, so that we may be able to comfort those who are in any affliction, with the comfort with which we ourselves are comforted by God. For as we share abundantly in Christ's sufferings, so through Christ we share abundantly in comfort too. (*II Corinthians 1:3–5*)

Key Ideas: Comfort from God
Our ministry of comfort
Suffering and comfort with Christ

Action Step: Visit or write a note to a friend who has recently begun to experience sorrow or grief; express your own view of the Christian hope.

Prayer: I do not always know the right words to say, Lord, but I will be myself today and do my best to encourage another.

206 FAITH WITH FRAGRANCE

But thanks be to God, who in Christ always leads us in triumph, and through us spreads the fragrance of the knowledge of him everywhere. For we are the aroma of Christ to God among those who are being saved and among those who are perishing, to one a fragrance from death to death, to the other a fragrance from life to life. Who is sufficient for these things? For we are not, like so many, peddlers of God's word; but as men of sincerity, as commissioned by God, in the sight of God we speak in Christ. (*II Corinthians 2:14–17*)

Key Ideas: Aromatic evangelism
A matter of life or death
Straightforward preaching

Action Step: Go forth to meet people with the conviction that your Christian faith holds the indispensable spiritual nourishment every human being in this world needs.

Prayer: It is the highest of privileges, Lord, that today You have chosen to use me as a bearer of the living Christ to others.

207 NEW COVENANT CONFIDENCE

You yourselves are our letter of recommendation, written on your hearts, to be known and read by all men; and you show that you are a letter from Christ delivered by us, written not with ink but with the Spirit of the living God, not on tablets of stone but on tablets of human hearts. Such is the confidence that we have through Christ toward God. Not that we are competent of ourselves to claim anything as coming from us; our competence is from God, who has made us competent to be ministers of a new covenant, not in a written code but in the Spirit; for the written code kills, but the Spirit gives life. (*II Corinthians 3:2–6*)

Key Ideas: Living letters for all to read
God is our Enabler
Ours is a life-giving religion

Action Step: Start living and working now with those qualities by which you may want a friend or associate to describe you later on in a letter of reference.

Prayer: Today, Lord, I'm going to be a good personal letter of reference for Jesus Christ.

208 THE TRANSFORMING VISION

Since we have such a hope, we are very bold, not like Moses, who put a veil over his face so that the Israelites might not see the end of the fading splendor. But their minds were hardened; for to this day, when they read the old covenant, that same veil remains unlifted, because only through Christ is it taken away. Yes, to this day whenever Moses is read a veil lies over their minds; but when a man turns to the Lord the veil is removed. Now the Lord is the Spirit, and where the Spirit of the Lord is, there is freedom. And we all, with unveiled face, beholding the glory of the Lord, are being changed into his likeness from one degree of glory to another; for this comes from the Lord who is the Spirit. (*II Corinthians 3:12–18*)

Key Ideas: The Spirit of splendor
The Spirit of freedom
The Spirit of renewal

Action Step: Review in the Gospel accounts Jesus' nonlegalistic way of living with the spiritual laws of the Old Testament concerning, for instance, the Sabbath, food, cleansing laws, and so forth.

Prayer: Help me to soar like a bird today, Lord, allowing Your Spirit to uphold and direct my flight.

209 TREASURE IN EARTHEN VESSELS

For what we preach is not ourselves, but Jesus Christ as Lord, with ourselves as your servants for Jesus' sake. For it is the God who said, "Let light shine out of darkness," who has shone in our hearts to give the light of the knowledge of the glory of God in the face of Christ. But we have this treasure in earthen vessels, to show that the transcendent power belongs to God and not to us. We are afflicted in every way, but not crushed; preplexed, but not driven to despair; persecuted, but not forsaken; struck down, but not destroyed; always carrying in the body the death of Jesus, so that the life of Jesus may also be manifested in our bodies. (*II Corinthians 4:5–10*)

Key Ideas: God's human face
God's power over us
God's Son in us

Action Step: Challenge members of your church (a class, circle of friends, or special prayer group) to pray regularly that your pastor may boldly and with power proclaim the message of Christ.

Prayer: I am so glad to know today, Lord, that I do not have to put on an appearance of being perfect as a Christian.

210 OUR ETERNAL HOME

So we do not lose heart. Though our outer nature is wasting away, our inner nature is being renewed every day. For this slight momentary affliction is preparing for us an eternal weight of glory beyond all comparison, because we look not to the things that are seen but to the things that are unseen; for the things that are seen are transient, but the things that are unseen are eternal. For we know that if the earthly tent we live in is destroyed, we have a building from God, a house not made with hands, eternal in the heavens. Here indeed we groan, and long to put on our heavenly dwelling, so that by putting it on we may not be found naked. For while we are still in this tent, we sigh with anxiety; not that we would be unclothed, but that we would be further clothed, so that what is mortal may be swallowed up by life. He who has prepared us for this very thing is God, who has given us the Spirit as a guarantee. So we are always of good courage; we know that while we are at home in the body we are away from the Lord, for we walk by faith, not by sight. We are of good courage, and we would rather be away from the body and at home with the Lord. So whether we are at home or away, we make it our aim to please him. For we must all appear before the judgment seat of Christ, so that each one may receive good or evil, according to what he has done in the body. (*II Corinthians 4:16–5:10*)

Key Ideas: Seeing the unseen
The heavenly reconstruction project
Advanced reservations

Action Step: Start reorganizing your life and values as if you will die someday; if some things need to be discarded, ask yourself, "What is there about my life that is presently a worthy investment for unending tomorrows?"

Prayer: Today, Lord, I will look with eyes of faith for the invisible realities in the changing world all around me.

211 OUR MINISTRY OF RECONCILIATION

For the love of Christ controls us, because we are convinced that one has died for all; therefore all have died. And he died for all, that those who live might live no longer for themselves but for him who for their sake died and was raised. From now on, therefore, we regard no one from a human point of view; even though we once regarded Christ from a human point of view, we regard him thus no longer. Therefore, if any one is in Christ, he is a new creation; the old has passed away, behold, the new has come. All this is from God, who through Christ reconciled us to himself and gave us the ministry of reconciliation; that is, in Christ God was reconciling the world to himself, not counting their trespasses against them, and entrusting to us the message of reconciliation. So we are ambassadors for Christ, God making his appeal through us. We beseech you on behalf of Christ, be reconciled to God. (*II Corinthians 5:14–20*)

Key Ideas: The master Christian motive
God's new creations
Ambassadors for God

Action Step: Show someone in a very practical way what it is like to be controlled by Jesus' unselfish love.

Prayer: I feel it a great honor today, Lord, to be given the assignment of being Your ambassador to every person in the world I meet.

212 CHRISTIAN CREDENTIALS

We put no obstacle in any one's way, so that no fault may be found with our ministry, but as servants of God we commend ourselves in every way: through great endurance, in afflictions, hardships, calamities, beatings, imprisonments, tumults, labors, watching, hunger; by purity, knowledge, forbearance, kindness, the Holy Spirit, genuine love, truthful speech, and the power of God; with the weapons of righteousness for the right hand and for the left; in honor and dishonor, in ill repute and good repute. We are treated as impostors, and yet are true; as unknown, and yet well known; as dying, and behold we live; as punished, and yet not killed; as sorrowful, yet always rejoicing; as poor, yet making many rich; as having nothing, and yet possessing everything. (*II Corinthians 6:3–10*)

Key Ideas: Servants of God through suffering
A Christian's positive warfare
Victory in spite of everything

Action Step: Make clear the intentions of your life as a Christian by proving by your actions the integrity of your motivations.

Prayer: Today, Lord, I know You can use whatever adversity or advantage occurs in my life to bless the world.

213 CHOICES IN GRIEF

For godly grief produces a repentance that leads to salvation and brings no regret, but worldly grief produces death. For see what earnestness this godly grief has produced in you, what eagerness to clear yourselves, what indignation, what alarm, what longing, what zeal, what punishment! (*II Corinthians 7:10, 11*)

Key Ideas: Godly grief
Bad grief
Good grief

Action Step: Help some friends to move into constructive expressions of grief that will give them a greater sensitivity for the needs and hurts of others.

Prayer: Lead me today, Lord, so that whatever the depths of my hurt, pain, or loss I may move into a new future strengthened within to serve You.

214 SPIRITUAL WEALTH

For you know the grace of our Lord Jesus Christ, that though he was rich, yet for your sake he became poor, so that by his poverty you might become rich. (*II Corinthians 8:9*)

Key Ideas: The lavish love of Christ
God reached our deepest need
Toward a new-fashioned wealth

Action Step: Name some of the treasures of the Christian faith to you; decide how you might invest these in the lives of others who are not yet spiritually wealthy.

Prayer: Lord, there are times when I feel poor in spirit before the ideal You have inspired in me, but today I am rich with the promise of a better life.

215 ABUNDANT GIVING AND LIVING

The point is this: he who sows sparingly will also reap sparingly, and he who sows bountifully will also reap bountifully. Each one must do as he has made up his mind, not reluctantly or under compulsion, for God loves a cheerful giver. And God is able to provide you with every blessing in abundance, so that you may always have enough of everything and may provide in abundance for every good work. As it is written,

> He scatters abroad, he gives to the poor; his righteousness endures forever.

He who supplies seed to the sower and bread for food will supply and multiply your resources and increase the harvest of your righteousness. You will be enriched in every way for great generosity, which through us will produce thanksgiving to God; for the rendering of this service not only supplies the wants of the saints but also overflows in many thanksgivings to God. Under the test of this service, you will glorify God by your obedience in acknowledging the gospel of Christ, and by the generosity of your contribution for them and for all others; while they long for you and pray for you, because of the surpassing grace of God in you. Thanks be to God for his inexpressible gift! (*II Corinthians 9:6–15*)

Key Ideas: The fruitful life of giving
The generating power of generosity
The Gospel of Christ in action

Action Step: Take a new and significant step forward toward sharing 10 percent of your financial resources in the mission and work of the Church.

Prayer: Since my heart is overflowing today with thanksgiving, Lord, help me to express this joy with overflowing stewardship as well.

216 CHRISTIAN CONFRONTATION

For though we live in the world we are not carrying on a worldly war, for the weapons of our warfare are not worldly but have divine power to destroy strongholds. We destroy arguments and every proud obstacle to the knowledge of God, and take every thought captive to obey Christ. (*II Corinthians 10:3–5*)

Key Ideas: New weapons for an old war
Our methods are guided by the Holy Spirit
Encountering intellect for Christ

Action Step: Enter into a fresh study of the Christian faith—its foundation and basic principles—with the same intensity and spirit of a modern research scientist.

Prayer: Today, Lord, I will accept truth without prejudice whenever and wherever it is said and whoever says it.

217 ADVENTURING WITH CHRIST

Five times I have received at the hands of the Jews the forty lashes less one. Three times I have been beaten with rods; once I was stoned. Three times I have been shipwrecked; a night and a day I have been adrift at sea; on frequent journeys, in danger from rivers, danger from robbers, danger from my own people, danger from Gentiles, danger in the city, danger in the wilderness, danger at sea, danger from false brethren; in toil and hardship, through many a sleepless night, in hunger and thirst, often without food, in cold and exposure. And, apart from other things, there is the daily pressure upon me of my anxiety for all the churches. Who is weak, and I am not weak? Who is made to fall, and I am not indignant? (*II Corinthians 11:24–29*)

Key Ideas: The courage required of missionaries
Dangers an apostle faced
Continuing concerns for the Church

Action Step: Review (in church journals, secular press, inquiries with the overseas mission offices) the kinds of persecutions Christians are now experiencing throughout the world.

Prayer: Because I am obligated to carry my part of the work of the Church, I will not ask today, Lord, to be exempt from problems that must be faced by those who are seeking to be faithful witnesses for the Christ.

218 STRENGTH IN OUR WEAKNESS

And to keep me from being too elated by the abundance of revelations, a thorn was given me in the flesh, a messenger of Satan, to harass me, to keep me from being too elated. Three times I besought the Lord about this, that it should leave me; but he said to me, "My grace is sufficient for you, for my power is made perfect in weakness." I will all the more gladly boast of my weaknesses, that the power of Christ may rest upon me. For the sake of Christ, then, I am content with weaknesses, insults, hardships, persecutions, and calamities; for when I am weak, then I am strong. (*II Corinthians 12:7–10*)

Key Ideas: Troubles often spark spiritual growth
Genuine prayer is a dialogue
A strange route to strength

Action Step: Recall some of the black spiritual songs; sing along with them about the faith we can have in the midst of suffering.

Prayer: Lord, if I get to the end of my rope today, I know You will be holding onto me even if I can no longer hold on myself.

219 CHRISTIAN SELF-EVALUATION

Examine yourselves, to see whether you are holding to your faith. Test yourselves. Do you not realize that Jesus Christ is in you?—unless indeed you fail to meet the test! (*II Corinthians 13:5*)

Key Ideas: Taking our spiritual temperature
Beware of fumbling your faith
The final proof of resurrection

Action Step: Alongside the great creeds and confessions of the Christian faith, describe the marks of the presence of the living Christ in the believer.

Prayer: Lord, today I treasure the opportunity to be developing a personal faith of my own, even though I realize I cannot rest in easy security.

220 A THREEFOLD BENEDICTION

The grace of the Lord Jesus Christ and the love of God and the fellowship of the Holy Spirit be with you all. (*II Corinthians 13:14*)

Key Ideas: The graceful Christ
The God who is love
The sharing Holy Spirit

Action Step: Read a good book on Christian worship, and discover what features make up meaningful and celebrative worship.

Prayer: Lord, I gratefully live today in the mystery of Your threefold self-expression of love.

221 STANDING FIRM

But because of false brethren secretly brought in, who slipped in to spy out our freedom which we have in Christ Jesus, that they might bring us into bondage—to them we did not yield submission even for a moment, that the truth of the gospel might be preserved for you. (*Galatians 2:4, 5*)

Key Ideas: Harassment is a hard test
Guarding our freedom
Hold to your convictions

Action Step: Stand up for what is right but make sure it is a big issue and not just a difference over opinions or methods.

Prayer: Lord, in my effort to be tolerant today, give me wisdom when and how to be firm about the essentials of the Christian faith.

222 CRUCIFIED WITH CHRIST

I have been crucified with Christ; it is no longer I who live, but Christ who lives in me; and the life I now live in the flesh I live by faith in the Son of God, who loved me and gave himself for me. I do not nullify the grace of God; for if justification were through the law, then Christ died to no purpose. (*Galatians 2:20, 21*)

Key Ideas: A new person in Christ
A life of faith with Christ
The love of Christ is our goal

Action Step: Work on some personal character trait which will bring your life into closer conformity to the mind and Spirit of Jesus.

Prayer: Lord, I can believe in a renewed world today because You are leading me into a renewed personality.

223 UNITY WITH DIFFERENCES

So that the law was our custodian until Christ came, that we might be justified by faith. But now that faith has come, we are no longer under a custodian; for in Christ Jesus you are all sons of God, through faith. For as many of you as were baptized into Christ have put on Christ. There is neither Jew nor Greek, there is neither slave nor free, there is neither male nor female; for you are all one in Christ Jesus. (*Galatians 3:24–28*)

Key Ideas: Growing up with faith
Baptism identifies us with Christ
Drawn into a new humanity

Action Step: Look in the mirror—real or imaginary—and ask yourself how your personality is wearing Christ Jesus as a life style.

Prayer: Lord, because of You I am able to greet my friends and fellow workers today with respect as gentlemen and gentlewomen.

224 HIS MISSION TO US

But when the time had fully come, God sent forth his Son, born of woman, born under the law, to redeem those who were under the law, so that we might receive adoption as sons. And because you are sons, God has sent the Spirit of his Son into our hearts, crying, "Abba! Father!" So through God you are no longer a slave but a son, and if a son then an heir. (*Galatians 4:4–7*)

Key Ideas: Chosen to be one with us
Who we were meant to be
Freed for communion with God

Action Step: Begin work on some unique expression or symbol of Christmas; utilize it then in your next Christmas greeting or contribution to your church's seasonal celebration.

Prayer: Since I sometimes drift into despair, Lord, I need the comfort today of knowing Your long-term purpose in Christ will not be subverted by any powers in this world.

225 FREEDOM'S WAY

For you were called to freedom, brethren; only do not use your freedom as an opportunity for the flesh, but through love be servants of one another. For the whole law is fulfilled in one word, "You shall love your neighbor as yourself." But if you bite and devour one another take heed that you are not consumed by one another. (*Galatians 5:13–15*)

Key Ideas: Responsibility is the twin of freedom
The spirit of the law is primary
Self-respect is essential to love

Action Step: Offer to do some task in and through your church that is essential even if it will not be noticed by many people.

Prayer: I am not sure whether I am really free to serve others today, Lord, but I want to be.

226 FRUITS OF THE SPIRIT

Now the works of the flesh are plain: fornication, impurity, licentiousness, idolatry, sorcery, enmity, strife, jealousy, anger, selfishness, dissension, party spirit, envy, drunkenness, carousing, and the like. I warn you, as I warned you before, that those who do such things shall not inherit the kingdom of God. But the fruit of the Spirit is love, joy, peace, patience, kindness, goodness, faithfulness, gentleness, self-control; against such there is no law. And those who belong to Christ Jesus have crucified the flesh with its passions and desires. (*Galatians 5:19–24*)

Key Ideas: The egocentric way
The higher way
Death for the old self

Action Step: Offer spiritual fruitbaskets to others through a personality dedicated to displaying Christlike qualities.

Prayer: I am still struggling today, Lord, to keep my animal drives in balance by the higher way of Christlike humanness.

227 OUR BURDENS AND THEIRS

Brethren, if a man is overtaken in any trespass, you who are spiritual should restore him in a spirit of gentleness. Look to yourself, lest you too be tempted. Bear one another's burdens, and so fulfill the law of Christ. For if any one thinks he is something, when he is nothing, he deceives himself. But let each one test his own work, and then his reason to boast will be in himself alone and not in his neighbor. For each man will have to bear his own load. (*Galatians 6:1–5*)

Key Ideas: In the struggle together
The duty of caring for others
Our individual responsibility

Action Step: Challenge your church to develop programs and approaches to ministry with people in need that are based upon respect for their abilities and that ensure they maintain their personal dignity.

Prayer: Lord, I will be a center of strength today for some troubled friend.

228 SOWING AND REAPING

Do not be deceived; God is not mocked, for whatever a man sows, that he will also reap. For he who sows to his own flesh will from the flesh reap corruption; but he who sows to the Spirit will from the Spirit reap eternal life. And let us not grow weary in well-doing, for in due season we shall reap, if we do not lose heart. (*Galatians 6:7–9*)

Key Ideas: Our wide-awake God
The law of the Spirit
Never give up on God

Action Step: Think carefully over your activities in the last month; measure how casually or seriously you are engaged in Christian good works.

Prayer: Lord, I am giving myself to cultivating creative good will today, and I am assured of a good harvest because of Your great faithfulness.

229 HIS CROSS AND OURS

For even those who receive circumcision do not themselves keep the law, but they desire to have you circumcised that they may glory in your flesh. But far be it from me to glory except in the cross of our Lord Jesus Christ, by which the world has been crucified to me, and I to the world. For neither is circumcision anything, nor uncircumcision, but a new creation. Peace and mercy be upon all who walk by this rule, upon the Israel of God. (*Galatians 6:13–16*)

Key Ideas: A new center of pride
A new view of the world
A new creation

Action Step: Construct a series of banners for the Lenten season utilizing some of the classical symbols of the cross.

Prayer: Lord, it has become clear to me today that the Christ gave Himself not to exempt me from the cross but to call me to a cruciform style of life.

230 THE PURPOSE OF GOD

Blessed be the God and Father of our Lord Jesus Christ, who has blessed us in Christ with every spiritual blessing in the heavenly places, even as he chose us in him before the foundation of the world, that we should be holy and blameless before him. He destined us in love to be his sons through Jesus Christ, according to the purpose of his will, to the praise of his glorious grace which he freely bestowed on us in the Beloved. In him we have redemption through his blood, the forgiveness of our trespasses, according to the riches of his grace which he lavished upon us. For he has made known to us in all wisdom and insight the mystery of his will, according to his purpose which he set forth in Christ as a plan for the fullness of time, to unite all things in him, things in heaven and things on earth. (*Ephesians 1:3–10*)

Key Ideas: Created to be God's children
A second chance
Christ—the key to our unity

Action Step: Attend a meeting for the rehabilitation of alcoholics; learn about the first steps the alcoholics agree to follow if they are to find hope for a better life.

Prayer: Lord, keep me dissatisfied today and always until I claim the good life and spiritual blessings You have promised all of Your children.

231 AMAZING GRACE

But God, who is rich in mercy, out of the great love with which he loved us, even when we were dead through our trespasses, made us alive together with Christ (by grace you have been saved), and raised us up with him, and made us sit with him in the heavenly places in Christ Jesus, that in the coming ages he might show the immeasurable riches of his grace in kindness toward us in Christ Jesus. For by grace you have been saved through faith; and this is not your own doing, it is the gift of God—not because of works, lest any man should boast. For we are his workmanship, created in Christ Jesus for good works, which God prepared beforehand, that we should walk in them. (*Ephesians 2:4–10*)

Key Ideas: The divine rescue mission
Salvation is a gift
God's work and ours

Action Step: Create an atmosphere in your Christian fellowship that makes it clear that Christians are always under construction.

Prayer: Lord, lead me today by Your amazing grace into a greater willingness to work for what I already know to be justice and compassion.

232 UNITED AT THE CROSS

But now in Christ Jesus you who once were far off have been brought near in the blood of Christ. For he is our peace, who has made us both one, and has broken down the dividing wall of hostility, by abolishing in his flesh the law of commandments and ordinances, that he might create in himself one new man in place of the two, so making peace, and might reconcile us both to God in one body through the cross, thereby bringing the hostility to an end. And he came and preached peace to you who were far off and peace to those who were near; for through him we both have access in one Spirit to the Father. So then you are no longer strangers and sojourners, but you are fellow citizens with the saints and members of the household of God, built upon the foundation of the apostles and prophets, Christ Jesus himself being the chief cornerstone, in whom the whole structure is joined together and grows into a holy temple in the Lord; in whom you also are built into it for a dwelling place of God in the Spirit. (*Ephesians 2:13–22*)

Key Ideas: Christ's reconciling cross
Peace to insiders and outsiders
The fellowship of the Spirit

Action Step: Propose a cooperative Christian Communion (Lord's Supper or Eucharist) service with another Christian fellowship in your community.

Prayer: Lord, make me a Christian bridge builder today who draws people together rather than a person who creates chasms.

233 CHRIST WITHIN US

For this reason I bow my knees before the Father, from whom every family in heaven and on earth is named, that according to the riches of his glory he may grant you to be strengthened with might through his Spirit in the inner man, and that Christ may dwell in your hearts through faith; that you, being rooted and grounded in love, may have power to comprehend with all the saints what is the breadth and length and height and depth, and to know the love of Christ which surpasses knowledge, that you may be filled with all the fullness of God. Now to him who by the power at work within us is able to do far more abundantly than all that we ask or think, to him be glory in the church and in Christ Jesus to all generations, for ever and ever. Amen. (*Ephesians 3:14–21*)

Key Ideas: Spiritual might within
Love that leads to fullness
Expanded horizons

Action Step: Reconsider initiating a worthwhile and creative project in your community organization or church of which others have said, "It can't be done"; try a faith experiment.

Prayer: Lord, I'm going to reach beyond the easy and convenient programs today to take up a task that calls forth greater faith.

234 OUR COMMON FAITH

I therefore, a prisoner for the Lord, beg you to lead a life worthy of the calling to which you have been called, with all lowliness and meekness, with patience, forbearing one another in love, eager to maintain the unity of the Spirit in the bond of peace. There is one body and one Spirit, just as you were called to the one hope that belongs to your call, one Lord, one faith, one baptism, one God and Father of us all, who is above all and through all and in all. (*Ephesians 4:1–6*)

Key Ideas: Life to match our faith
Faith with love
Faith that unites us

Action Step: Plan a community event or action project in which Christians of various fellowships and denominations may witness to their common faith.

Prayer: Lord, in my desire to be loyal to the faith today I want to respect the liberty of opinions of those with whom I differ.

235 GIFTS THAT MATTER

And his gifts were that some should be apostles, some prophets, some evangelists, some pastors and teachers, to equip the saints for the work of ministry, for building up the body of Christ, until we all attain to the unity of the faith and of the knowledge of the Son of God, to mature manhood, to the measure of the stature of the fulness of Christ; so that we may no longer be children, tossed to and fro and carried about with every wind of doctrine, by the cunning of men, by their craftiness in deceitful wiles. Rather, speaking the truth in love, we are to grow up in every way into him who is the head, into Christ, from whom the whole body, joined and knit together by every joint with which it is supplied, when each part is working properly, makes bodily growth and upbuilds itself in love. (*Ephesians 4:11–16*)

Key Ideas: Personal growth in Christ
Discerning religious manipulators
A fellowship for growth

Action Step: Enroll in a short-term leader development study course on Bible study, church mission directions, or something similar that will require some hard work and thinking.

Prayer: Show me today, Lord, the ministry I am called to engage in with all Christians.

236 TRUTHFULNESS AND TENDERNESS

Therefore, putting away falsehood, let every one speak the truth with his neighbor, for we are members one of another. Be angry but do not sin; do not let the sun go down on your anger, and give no opportunity to the devil. Let the thief no longer steal, but rather let him labor, doing honest work with his hands, so that he may be able to give to those in need. Let no evil talk come out of your mouths, but only such as is good for edifying, as fits the occasion, that it may impart grace to those who hear. And do not grieve the Holy Spirit of God, in whom you were sealed for the day of redemption. Let all bitterness and wrath and anger and clamor and slander be put away from you, with all malice, and be kind to one another, tenderhearted, forgiving one another, as God in Christ forgave you. (*Ephesians 4:25–32*)

Key Ideas: Closing the door to the devil
God as our friendly Guest
Forgiving as we are forgiven

Action Step: Check your style of speech; perhaps your associates and friends can be encouraged even by the way you make requests and demands.

Prayer: Before today is over, Lord, I hope to deal with whatever anger and hostility that are inflicting hurt to my soul as well as to others.

237 SOBER BUT SPIRITED

Awake, O sleeper, and arise from the dead, and Christ shall give you light.

Look carefully then how you walk, not as unwise men but as wise, making the most of the time, because the days are evil. Therefore do not be foolish, but understand what the will of the Lord is. And do not get drunk with wine, for that is debauchery; but be filled with the Spirit, addressing one another in psalms and hymns and spiritual songs, singing and making melody to the Lord with all your heart, always and for everything giving thanks in the name of our Lord Jesus Christ to God the Father. *(Ephesians 5:14–20)*

Key Ideas: Waking up to the light
Drinking deeply of the Spirit
Singing our faith with thanksgiving

Action Step: Spend some time with your church hymnal—alone or in a course on hymnology; try to compose a hymn for our times.

Prayer: Lord, I know that however awake I may be today, You are always awake before me.

238 LOYALTY AND LOVE

Be subject to one another out of reverence for Christ. Wives, be subject to your husbands, as to the Lord. For the husband is the head of the wife as Christ is the head of the church, his body, and is himself its Savior. As the church is subject to Christ, so let wives also be subject in everything to their husbands. Husbands, love your wives, as Christ loved the church and gave himself up for her, that he might consecrate her, having cleansed her by the washing of water with the word, that the church might be presented before him in splendor, without spot or wrinkle or any such thing, that she might be holy and without blemish. Even so husbands should love their wives as their own bodies. He who loves his wife loves himself. For no man ever hates his own flesh, but nourishes and cherishes it, as Christ does the church, because we are members of his body. "For this reason a man shall leave his father and mother and be joined to his wife, and the two shall become one flesh." This mystery is a profound one, and I am saying that it refers to Christ and the church, however, let each one of you love his wife as himself, and let the wife see that she respects her husband. (*Ephesians 5:21–33*)

Key Ideas: Christ's perfect love
Christ's hope for the Church
Christ's oneness with us

Action Step: Surprise your husband or your wife (or a couple who are friends) with some sign of appreciation for their grace and thoughtfulness or acceptance of special responsibilities.

Prayer: I rejoice today, Lord, because You have given us the intimacy of loyalty and love in marriage.

239 FAMILY COVENANT

Children, obey your parents in the Lord, for this is right. "Honor your father and mother" (this is the first commandment with a promise), "that it may be well with you and that you may live long on the earth." Fathers, do not provoke your children to anger, but bring them up in the discipline and instruction of the Lord. (*Ephesians 6:1–4*)

Key Ideas: Respect for your parents
Hope for a happy family
Respect for your children

Action Step: Establish the channels of family communications in the sunshine days so that you may be able to cope with the pressures of the cloudy days of conflict or estrangement.

Prayer: Lord, I will treasure these precious hours of today and not let them end before I say "I love you" to those very dear to me.

240 THE WHOLE ARMOR OF GOD

Finally, be strong in the Lord and in the strength of his might. Put on the whole armor of God, that you may be able to stand against the wiles of the devil. For we are not contending against flesh and blood, but against the principalities, against the powers, against the world rulers of this present darkness, against the spiritual hosts of wickedness in the heavenly places. Therefore take the whole armor of God, that you may be able to withstand in the evil day, and having done all, to stand. Stand therefore, having girded your loins with truth, and having put on the breastplate of righteousness, and having shod your feet with the equipment of the gospel of peace; besides all of these taking the shield of faith, with which you can quench all the flaming darts of the evil one. And take the helmet of salvation, and the sword of the Spirit, which is the word of God. (*Ephesians 6:10–17*)

Key Ideas: Enlightened against evil
Enabled for endurance
Equipped for encounter

Action Step: Study the biographies of some courageous saints; look for the secret of the toughness of their faith.

Prayer: Lord, strengthen me today for seeing the world in its stark reality of evil as well as good.

241 OUR CHRISTIAN NEIGHBORS

Some indeed preach Christ from envy and rivalry, but others from good will. The latter do it out of love, knowing that I am put here for the defense of the gospel; the former proclaim Christ out of partisanship, not sincerely but thinking to afflict me in my imprisonment. What then? Only that in every way, whether in pretense or in truth, Christ is proclaimed; and in that I rejoice. (*Philippians 1:15–18*)

Key Ideas: Preaching Christ in His Spirit
Presenting a narrow Christ
God works sometimes in spite of us

Action Step: Actively support some cooperative Christian project or organization demonstrating your trust in the mutual ministry with other Christians.

Prayer: Today when others are competitive with their Christianity, Lord, keep me fair and generous with Your wisdom.

242 LIVING MEANS CHRIST

Yes, and I shall rejoice. For I know that through your prayers and the help of the Spirit of Jesus Christ this will turn out for my deliverance, as it is my eager expectation and hope that I shall not be at all ashamed, but that with full courage now as always Christ will be honored in my body, whether by life or by death. For to me to live is Christ, and to die is gain. If it is to be life in the flesh, that means fruitful labor for me. Yet which I shall choose I cannot tell. I am hard pressed between the two. My desire is to depart and be with Christ, for that is far better. But to remain in the flesh is more necessary on your account. (*Philippians 1:19–24*)

Key Ideas: Trusting Christ in trouble
Courage to die for Christ
Willingness to live with Him

Action Step: Make a list of several reasons you have for living; number them in order of their priority.

Prayer: Whatever restrictions I face today, Lord, I am determined not to let them get me down.

243 THE MIND OF CHRIST

Do nothing from selfishness or conceit, but in humility count others better than yourselves. Let each of you look not only to his own interests, but also to the interests of others. Have this mind among yourselves, which is yours in Christ Jesus, who, though he was in the form of God, did not count equality with God a thing to be grasped, but emptied himself, taking the form of a servant, being born in the likeness of men. And being found in human form he humbled himself and became obedient unto death, even death on a cross. Therefore God has highly exalted him and bestowed on him the name which is above every name, that at the name of Jesus every knee should bow, in heaven and on earth and under the earth, and every tongue confess that Jesus Christ is Lord, to the glory of God the Father. (*Philippians 2:3–11*)

Key Ideas: The right regard of others
God's model for human life
The grand reversal of authority

Action Step: Among the leadership positions you hold commit yourself to seeking and claiming authority only as it is earned by service.

Prayer: Lord, I am going to live responsibly toward You even if I cannot expect everything to be 100 percent to my advantage today.

244 FLAMBOYANT FAITH

Work out your own salvation with fear and trembling; for God is at work in you, both to will and to work for his good pleasure. Do all things without grumbling or questioning, that you may be blameless and innocent, children of God without blemish in the midst of a crooked and perverse generation, among whom you shine as lights in the world, holding fast the word of life, so that in the day of Christ I may be proud that I did not run in vain or labor in vain. (*Philippians 2:12–16*)

Key Ideas: God is in our work
Keeping a positive perspective
A faith that illumines

Action Step: Treat your regular associates with an intense respect for their ability to cope with the work and frustrations they face.

Prayer: Lord, I want to be an expression of Christianity for today that is both warm and enlightening.

245 THE GAIN CHRIST GIVES

But whatever gain I had, I counted as loss for the sake of Christ. Indeed I count everything as loss because of the surpassing worth of knowing Christ Jesus my Lord. For his sake I have suffered the loss of all things, and count them as refuse, in order that I may gain Christ and be found in him, not having a righteousness of my own, based on law, but that which is through faith in Christ, the righteousness from God that depends on faith; that I may know him and the power of his resurrection, and may share his sufferings, becoming like him in his death, that if possible I may attain the resurrection from the dead. (*Philippians 3:7–11*)

Key Ideas: The risk worth taking
The rightness God gives us
The resurrection is for now

Action Step: Evaluate your personal worth without the benefit of racial, social, or economic status symbols.

Prayer: Lord, I will be satisfied today with the rewards that only one's faith can bring.

246 THE UPWARD WAY

Not that I have already obtained this or am already perfect; but I press on to make it my own because Christ Jesus has made me his own. Brethren, I do not consider that I have made it my own; but one thing I do, forgetting what lies behind and straining forward to what lies ahead, I press on toward the goal for the prize of the upward call of God in Christ Jesus. Let those of us who are mature be thus minded; and if in anything you are otherwise minded, God will reveal that also to you. Only let us hold true to what we have attained. (*Philippians 3:12–16*)

Key Ideas: A healthy discontent
The forward look with Christ
Conserving our spiritual gains

Action Step: Start a program of positive self-development in some area of your life where your knowledge, abilities, or experience are inadequate.

Prayer: Help me, Lord, to stretch forward today in my spiritual mountain climbing, even if it is somewhat dangerous and painful.

247 REJOICING ANYWAY

Rejoice in the Lord always; again I will say, Rejoice. Let all men know your forbearance. The Lord is at hand. Have no anxiety about anything, but in everything by prayer and supplication with thanksgiving let your requests be made known to God. And the peace of God, which passes all understanding, will keep your hearts and your minds in Christ Jesus. (*Philippians 4:4–7*)

Key Ideas: A holy habit of joy
Practicing prayers of trust
Discovering a center of strength

Action Step: Turn over to God's control your worry over the outcome of your most pressing problem.

Prayer: Lord, I am able to rejoice about life today because of Your never-failing guidance.

248 VALID VALUES

Finally, brethren, whatever is true, whatever is honorable, whatever is just, whatever is pure, whatever is lovely, whatever is gracious, if there is any excellence, if there is anything worthy of praise, think about these things. What you have learned and received and heard and seen in me, do; and the God of peace will be with you. (*Philippians 4:8, 9*)

Key Ideas: Aiming for excellence
A thinking person for Jesus Christ
Living the truth

Action Step: Converse with a Christian teacher or mature friend on the process involved in Christlike thinking on questions and issues in our modern world.

Prayer: Lord, I want the doors of my intellect to swing inward and outward today.

249 READY FOR EVERYTHING

Not that I complain of want; for I have learned, in whatever state I am, to be content. I know how to be abased, and I know how to abound; in any and all circumstances I have learned the secret of facing plenty and hunger, abundance and want. I can do all things in him who strengthens me. (*Philippians 4:11–13*)

Key Ideas: Christian contentment
Education for adversity
Personal power for living

Action Step: Affirm boldly to someone your trust in the enabling power of Jesus Christ.

Prayer: I know, Lord, that I am a rich person today because of Your great grace.

250 CENTER AND CIRCUMFERENCE

He has delivered us from the dominion of darkness and transferred us to the kingdom of his beloved Son, in whom we have redemption, the forgiveness of sins. He is the image of the invisible God, the first-born of all creation; for in him all things were created, in heaven and on earth, visible and invisible, whether thrones or dominions or principalities or authorities—all things were created through him and for him. He is before all things, and in him all things hold together. He is the head of the body, the church; he is the beginning, the first-born from the dead, that in everything he might be preeminent. For in him all the fulness of God was pleased to dwell, and through him to reconcile to himself all things, whether on earth or in heaven, making peace by the blood of his cross. (*Colossians 1:13–20*)

Key Ideas: Christ, the Deliverer from darkness
Christ, the Center of creation
Christ, the Head of the Church

Action Step: Make a few notes indicating the ways that Jesus has brought deliverance into your personal life.

Prayer: Lord, today I am relieved that the Church has a perfectly adequate Leader, especially when I feel my many imperfections and limitations.

251 CHRIST FOR EVERYONE

I became a minister according to the divine office which was given to me for you, to make the word of God fully known, the mystery hidden for ages and generations but now made manifest to his saints. To them God chose to make known how great among the Gentiles are the riches of the glory of this mystery, which is Christ in you, the hope of glory. Him we proclaim, warning every man and teaching every man in all wisdom, that we may present every man mature in Christ. (*Colossians 1:25–28*)

Key Ideas: The mystery revealed
Christ lives in us
Nurture for everyone

Action Step: Encourage your minister to explain to your church the qualifications and preparations for the Christian ministry for our time.

Prayer: Today, Lord, I am going to look carefully for the possibilities of nurturing the Spirit of Christ in others.

252 STAYING TRUE

As therefore you received Christ Jesus the Lord, so live in him, rooted and built up in him and established in the faith, just as you were taught, abounding in thanksgiving. See to it that no one makes a prey of you by philosophy and empty deceit, according to human tradition, according to the elemental spirits of the universe, and not according to Christ. For in him dwells the whole fulness of deity bodily, and you have come to fulness of life in him, who is the head of all rule and authority. (*Colossians 2:6–10*)

Key Ideas: Roots that count
No substitutes for Christ
A full life with Christ

Action Step: To your family, some good friends, or some seekers of truth, explain what you consider to be the absolutely essential features of your Christian faith.

Prayer: Since You are the stability of my life, Lord, I am not going to fall prey today to every promoter of "spiritual" ideas.

253 RELIGION OF MATURITY

And you, who were dead in trespasses and the uncircumcision of your flesh, God made alive together with him, having forgiven us all our trespasses, having canceled the bond which stood against us with its legal demands; this he set aside, nailing it to the cross. He disarmed the principalities and powers and made a public example of them, triumphing over them in him. Therefore let no one pass judgment on you in questions of food and drink or with regard to a festival or a new moon or a sabbath. These are only a shadow of what is to come; but the substance belongs to Christ. Let no one disqualify you, insisting on self-abasement and worship of angels, taking his stand on visions, puffed up without reach by his sensuous mind, and not holding fast to the Head, from whom the whole body, nourished and knit together through its joints and ligaments, grows with a growth that is from God. (*Colossians 2:13–19*)

Key Ideas: Christ liberated us for life
Guard your freedom in Christ
The key to Christian growth

Action Step: Review with Christian friends the basic New Testament principles that reflect the Spirit of Jesus Christ in deciding what is right and wrong.

Prayer: Lord, I thank You that I am able to explore the fulness of the Gospel today without fear of intimidation from self-appointed spiritual experts.

254 BEYOND OLD WAYS

If then you have been raised with Christ, seek the things that are above, where Christ is, seated at the right hand of God. Set your minds on things that are above, not on things that are on earth. For you have died, and your life is hid with Christ in God. When Christ who is our life appears, then you also will appear with him in glory. Put to death therefore what is earthly in you: fornication, impurity, passion, evil desire, and covetousness, which is idolatry. On account of these the wrath of God is coming upon the sons of disobedience, among whom you also once walked, when you lived in these things. But now put away also all these: anger, wrath, malice, slander, and foul talk from your mouth. Do not lie to one another, seeing that you have put off the old nature with its practices and have put on the new nature, which is being renewed in knowledge after the image of its creator. Here there cannot be Greek and Jew, circumcised and uncircumcised, barbarian, Scythian, slave, free man, but Christ is all, and in all. (*Colossians 3:1–11*)

Key Ideas: A heavenly life for now
Hope of lasting life with Christ
Death to sins in particular

Action Step: Look carefully at your community's various value systems, asking, "Can we as Christians seek out, confront, and inspire to a new life persons who are destroying themselves?"

Prayer: Lord, with Your guidance today I can soar to new heights of living and hope.

255 CHRIST WITHIN

Put on then, as God's chosen ones, holy and beloved, compassion, kindness, lowliness, meekness, and patience, forbearing one another and, if one has a complaint against another, forgiving each other; as the Lord has forgiven you, so you also must forgive. And above all these put on love, which binds everything together in perfect harmony. And let the peace of Christ rule in your hearts, to which indeed you were called in the one body. And be thankful. Let the word of Christ dwell in you richly, teach and admonish one another in all wisdom, and sing psalms and hymns and spiritual songs with thankfulness in your hearts to God. And whatever you do, in word or deed, do everything in the name of the Lord Jesus, giving thanks to God the Father through him. (*Colossians 3:12–17*)

Key Ideas: The new Christian life style
The centrifugal force of Christ's love
The enabling Word of Christ

Action Step: Do something whimsical, ridiculous, or hilarious with some close friend(s) that expresses the joy of life.

Prayer: How beautiful it is today, Lord, to love and be loved by others!

256 CLEAR MOTIVES

For you yourselves know, brethren, that our visit to you was not in vain; but though we had already suffered and been shamefully treated at Philippi, as you know, we had courage in our God to declare to you the gospel of God in the face of great opposition. For our appeal does not spring from error or uncleanness, nor is it made with guile; but just as we have been approved by God to be entrusted with the gospel, so we speak, not to please men, but to please God who tests our hearts. For we never used either words of flattery, as you know, or a cloak for greed, as God is witness; nor did we seek glory from men, whether from you or from others, though we might have made demands as apostles of Christ. But we were gentle among you, like a nurse taking care of her children. So, being affectionately desirous of you, we were ready to share with you not only the gospel of God but also our own selves, because you had become very dear to us. (*I Thessalonians 2:1–8*)

Key Ideas: Authority for ministry
Motives matter in Christian service
The personal touch in caring

Action Step: Enter into a discussion with Christian friends, perhaps with your minister present, on what constitutes a "call" to the ministry as a life vocation in the Church.

Prayer: Lord, I want to work with people today for the right reasons.

257 THE MARRIAGE RELATIONSHIP

For this is the will of God, your consecration: that you abstain from unchastity that each one of you know how to take a wife for himself or how to control his own body in consecration and honor, not in the passion of lust like heathen who do not know God; that no man transgress, and wrong his brother in this matter, because the Lord is an avenger in all these things, as we solemnly forewarned you. For God has not called us for uncleanness, but in consecration. (*I Thessalonians 4:3–7*)

Key Ideas: Matching our behavior to our beliefs
Living on love versus lust
A soul cleansed for service

Action Step: If you are a husband or wife, consider how you may bring greater joy and fulfillment in the expression of your affections toward your spouse.

Prayer: Direct me today, Lord, in seeking the happiness of others first so that my own happiness will follow as You will it.

258 GRIEF AND RELIEF

But we would not have you ignorant, brethren, concerning those who are asleep, that you may not grieve as others do who have no hope. For since we believe that Jesus died and rose again, even so, through Jesus, God will bring with him those who have fallen asleep. For this we declare to you by the word of the Lord, that we who are alive, who are left until the coming of the Lord, shall not precede those who have fallen asleep. For the Lord himself will descend from heaven with a cry of command, with the archangel's call, and with the sound of the trumpet of God. And the dead in Christ will rise first; then we who are alive, who are left, shall be caught up together with them in the clouds to meet the Lord in the air; and so we shall always be with the Lord. Therefore comfort one another with these words. (*I Thessalonians 4:13–18*)

Key Ideas: Facing grief with hope
Meeting death with Christ
Faith for comforting others

Action Step: Do the work of waiting patiently for the final day of the Lord; be about spreading the Lord's good will for the world and leave the calendar watching to Him.

Prayer: Today, Lord, I refuse to be afraid of my dying, since I am sure You alone can guarantee my tomorrows.

259 CHILDREN OF LIGHT

For you are all sons of light and sons of the day; we are not of the night or of darkness. So then let us not sleep, as others do, but let us keep awake and be sober. For those who sleep sleep at night, and those who get drunk are drunk at night. But, since we belong to the day, let us be sober, and put on the breastplate of faith and love, and for a helmet the hope of salvation. For God has not destined us for wrath, but to obtain salvation through our Lord Jesus Christ, who died for us so that whether we wake or sleep we might live with him. (*I Thessalonians 5:5–10*)

Key Ideas: Alert and awake living
Equipped for daily action
God's goal for us

Action Step: Begin the day hopefully expectant that you will meet people and have experiences that are creative and fulfilling.

Prayer: What a beautiful and wonderful day You have given me today, Lord, in which to work and learn and give of myself!

260 CHRISTIAN COOPERATION

But we beseech you, brethren, to respect those who labor among you and are over you in the Lord and admonish you, and to esteem them very highly in love because of their work. Be at peace among yourselves. And we exhort you, brethren, admonish the idlers, encourage the fainthearted, help the weak, be patient with them all. See that none of you repays evil for evil, but always seek to do good to one another and to all. (*I Thessalonians 5:12–15*)

Key Ideas: Respecting good leaders
Everyone can do something
Positive action for others

Action Step: Find an appropriate way to convey encouragement and appreciation to your minister(s) and key leaders for their dedicated service to the Church.

Prayer: While I reach out with patient understanding toward others today, Lord, help me to always keep the goal of excellence held high before me.

261 THANKS IN ALL CIRCUMSTANCES

Rejoice always, pray constantly, give thanks in all circumstances; for this is the will of God in Christ Jesus for you. Do not quench the Spirit, do not despise prophesying, but test everything; hold fast what is good, abstain from every form of evil. (*I Thessalonians 5:16–22*)

Key Ideas: Celebrate life in God's presence
The Spirit can be stifled
Sorting out our values

Action Step: Try an experiment with all the people you meet this week; see whether they respond more enthusiastically when you smile than when you don't.

Prayer: Lord, I will be ready today for the fresh anointings.and breezes of Your Spirit.

262 OFFERING A BLESSING

Now may our Lord Jesus Christ himself, and God our Father, who loved us and gave us eternal comfort and good hope through grace, comfort your hearts and establish them in every good work and word. (*II Thessalonians 2:16, 17*)

Key Ideas: In the beginning is love
Living with the long view of hope
A down-to-earth religion

Action Step: Be quiet and listen to people; hold back your compulsive talking for a one-day or one-week experiment.

Prayer: Lord, transmit Your love today through me to persons who need hope.

263 GOD PRESENT AND LEADING

But the Lord is faithful; he will strengthen you and guard you from evil. And we have confidence in the Lord about you, that you are doing and will do the things which we command. May the Lord direct your hearts to the love of God and to the steadfastness of Christ. (*II Thessalonians 3:3–5*)

Key Ideas: Empowerment and protection from God
Leadership inspiring confidence
Divine model of love and loyalty

Action Step: Display your confidence and hope in others by requesting their help or delegating some significant responsibility to them.

Prayer: Lord, free me today from putting persons down while I am trying to build them up.

264 THE VALUE OF WORKING

If any one will not work, let him not eat. For we hear that some of you are living in idleness, mere busybodies, not doing any work. Now such persons we command and exhort in the Lord Jesus Christ to do their work in quietness and to earn their own living. Brethren, do not be weary in well-doing. (*II Thessalonians 3:10–13*)

Key Ideas: A stringent remedy for laziness
Learning to work for a living
Never give up doing good

Action Step: Find something to do—a job, chores, helping—to show you will do your share with your family or friends.

Prayer: Lord, when the sweat of my labor pours out today, it will be my spiritual offering to You.

265 SALVATION OF SINNERS

The saying is sure and worthy of full acceptance, that Christ Jesus came into the world to save sinners. And I am the foremost of sinners; but I received mercy for this reason, that in me, as the foremost, Jesus Christ might display his perfect patience for an example to those who were to believe in him for eternal life. To the King of ages, immortal, invisible, the only God, be honor and glory for ever and ever. Amen. *(I Timothy 1:15–17)*

Key Ideas: The primary mission of Jesus
Remembering where we have been
The power of a demonstration

Action Step: Help someone to become aware or to recall that the Church is a fellowship of forgiven sinners.

Prayer: I know today, Lord, that only by Your great grace will I be able to avoid the gravest of sins.

266 PRAYERS FOR PEACE

First of all, then, I urge that supplications, prayers, intercessions, and thanksgivings be made for all men, for kings and all who are in high positions, that we may lead a quiet and peaceable life, godly and respectful in every way. This is good, and it is acceptable in the sight of God our Savior, who desires all men to be saved and to come to the knowledge of the truth. For there is one God, and there is one mediator between God and men, the man Christ Jesus, who gave himself as a ransom for all, the testimony to which was borne at the proper time. *(I Timothy 2:1–6)*

Key Ideas: Prayer and action for a peaceful society
Salvation is experienced by knowledge
Christ in the middle

Action Step: Write a letter of commendation to a political official mentioning you are remembering him or her in your prayers.

Prayer: Lord, today make me into a bridge that unites people to people and to You.

267 SPIRITUAL LEADERS

The saying is sure: If anyone aspires to the office of bishop, he desires a noble task. Now a bishop must be above reproach, the husband of one wife, temperate, sensible, dignified, hospitable, an apt teacher, no drunkard, not violent but gentle, not quarrelsome, and no lover of money. He must manage his own household well, keeping his children submissive and respectful in every way; for if a man does not know how to manage his own household, how can he care for God's church? He must not be a recent convert, or he may be puffed up with conceit and fall into the condemnation of the devil; moreover he must be well thought of by outsiders, or he may fall into reproach and the snare of the devil. (*I Timothy 3:1–7*)

Key Ideas: Leadership with character
Leadership with experience
Leadership with humility

Action Step: Along with leadership skills advocate high moral and spiritual commitment for the lay and professional ministerial leadership of your church.

Prayer: I will strive today, Lord, to display in my own life some of those same qualities of life that I expect of all Christian leaders.

268 QUALIFIED SERVANTS

Deacons likewise must be serious, not double-tongued, not addicted to much wine, not greedy for gain; they must hold the mystery of the faith with a clear conscience. And let them also be tested first; then if they prove themselves blameless let them serve as deacons. The women likewise must be serious, no slanderers, but temperate, faithful in all things. Let deacons be the husband of one wife, and let them manage their children and their households well; for those who serve well as deacons gain a good standing for themselves and also great confidence in the faith which is in Christ Jesus. (*I Timothy 3:8–13*)

Key Ideas: Sincere servants
Proven servants
Growing servants

Action Step: Support the programs of lay and professional leadership training in your congregation or church denomination.

Prayer: Lord, spark me today to do some creative thing to show Christian leaders that I believe in their work.

269 THE MYSTERY OF OUR RELIGION

Great indeed, we confess, is the mystery of our religion:

He was manifested in the flesh,
vindicated in the Spirit,
  seen by angels,
preached among the nations,
believed on in the world,
  taken up in glory.

(I Timothy 3:16)

Key Ideas: The positive side of confession
The mystery made clear in Christ
The goal of God's Good News

Action Step: Briefly put down in your own words what you believe is the core of the Christian faith.

Prayer: Lord, make me bold today in my statements and demonstrations of the Christian faith.

270 GOD'S GOOD WORLD

Now the Spirit expressly says that in later times some will depart from the faith by giving heed to deceitful spirits and doctrines of demons, through the pretensions of liars whose consciences are seared, who forbid marriage and enjoin abstinence from foods which God created to be received with thanksgiving by those who believe and know the truth. For everything created by God is good, and nothing is to be rejected if it is received with thanksgiving; for then it is consecrated by the word of God and prayer. *(I Timothy 4:1–5)*

Key Ideas: The Spirit of Christ and demon spirits
Confusing the surface and the depths
The scope of Christian salvation

Action Step: Do something special for yourself that will allow you to celebrate being alive.

Prayer: Lord, keep me sober in my life and faith today, but please deliver me from stuffiness.

271 BODY AND SOUL

Train yourself in godliness; for while bodily training is of some value, godliness is of value in every way, as it holds promise for the present life and also for the life to come. The saying is sure and worthy of full acceptance. For to this end we toil and strive, because we have our hope set on the living God, who is the Savior of all men, especially of those who believe. (*I Timothy 4:7–10*)

Key Ideas: The wisdom of keeping physically fit
Health of the soul matters more
An agony inspired by hope

Action Step: Begin some form of regular physical exercise adjusted to your own physique and age.

Prayer: Lead me today, Lord, in the way of total health of body, spirit, and soul.

272 THE GIFT WITHIN YOU

Let no one despise your youth, but set the believers an example in speech and conduct, in love, in faith, in purity. Till I come, attend to the public reading of scripture, to preaching, to teaching. Do not neglect the gift you have, which was given you by prophetic utterance when the council of elders laid their hands upon you. Practice these duties, devote yourself to them, so that all may see your progress. Take heed to yourself and to your teaching; hold to that, for by so doing you will save both yourself and your hearers. (*I Timothy 4:12–16*)

Key Ideas: Authority and maturity
Developing skills for ministry
Starting with yourself

Action Step: Say something encouraging to a young person which expresses your belief in his or her efforts.

Prayer: Help me, Lord, to be faithful to my agreements and not to let anyone down who is counting on me today.

273 FAMILY RESPONSIBILITIES

If any one does not provide for his relatives, and especially for his own family, he has disowned the faith and is worse than an unbeliever. (*I Timothy 5:8*)

Key Ideas: True religion is a relative affair
The family working together
Ethical detours are dangerous

Action Step: Write a letter, call, or visit a member of your family letting them know of your concern for their welfare.

Prayer: Lord, watch over my loved ones today—those near and far away—for I cannot show my best concern without Your help.

274 CHRISTIAN CONTENTMENT

There is great gain in godliness with contentment; for we brought nothing into the world, and we cannot take anything out of the world; but if we have food and clothing, with these we shall be content. But those who desire to be rich fall into temptation, into a snare, into many senseless and hurtful desires that plunge men into ruin and destruction. For the love of money is the root of all evils; it is through this craving that some have wandered away from the faith and pierced their hearts with many pangs. (*I Timothy 6:6–10*)

Key Ideas: A life of spiritual affluence
The slippery slope of material success
When money is master

Action Step: Become a personal friend of someone on a lower economic scale than yourself; learn or relearn some more of the secrets of happiness.

Prayer: If all of my things washed, blew, or burned away today, Lord, I could make it tomorrow because of Your love.

275 THE GOOD CONFESSION

But as for you, man of God, shun all this; aim at righteousness, godliness, faith, love, steadfastness, gentleness. Fight the good fight of the faith; take hold of the eternal life to which you were called when you made the good confession in the presence of many witnesses. In the presence of God who gives life to all things, and of Christ Jesus who in his testimony before Pontius Pilate made the good confession, I charge you to keep the commandment unstained and free from reproach until the appearing of our Lord Jesus Christ; and this will be made manifest at the proper time by the blessed and only Sovereign, the King of kings and Lord of lords, who alone has immortality and dwells in unapproachable light, whom no man has ever seen or can see. To him be honor and eternal dominion. Amen. (*I Timothy 6:11–16*)

Key Ideas: Aim high for Christlike qualities
Courageous witnessing to the end
Christ is the end point of history

Action Step: Raise this question to your Christian friends: "How long have you been personally committed to and available for service in the Kingdom of God?"

Prayer: Lord, I treasure today as the highest of human privileges the freedom of deciding for or against Jesus as my Christ.

276 TWO KINDS OF RICHES

As for the rich in this world, charge them not to be haughty, nor to set their hopes on uncertain riches but on God who richly furnishes us with everything to enjoy. They are to do good, to be rich in good deeds, liberal and generous, thus laying up for themselves a good foundation for the future, so that they may take hold of the life which is life indeed. (*I Timothy 6:17–19*)

Key Ideas: The spiritual basis of enduring hope
The liberal spirit in action
The best retirement plan of all

Action Step: As an individual or in a family conference, evaluate your family spending, saving, and sharing with your church and other worthwhile causes.

Prayer: Lord, I intend to make my spending shape up to Your standards today.

277 CONTAGIOUS FAITH

I am reminded of your sincere faith, a faith that dwelt first in your grandmother Lois and your mother Eunice and now, I am sure, dwells in you. Hence I remind you to rekindle the gift of God that is within you through the laying on of my hands; for God did not give us a spirit of timidity but a spirit of power and love and self-control. (*II Timothy 1:5–7*)

Key Ideas: The torch of faith
Consecration in the community of faith
Personal gifts from God

Action Step: Do something positive and constructive—speak out, be present at a meeting, or go on record publicly—declaring your commitment to a Christian concept of the quality of life in your community.

Prayer: Help me, Lord, to keep the fire of faith burning today as others have before me.

278 A HOLY CALLING

Do not be ashamed then of testifying to our Lord, nor of me his prisoner, but share in suffering for the gospel in the power of God, who saved us and called us with a holy calling, not in virtue of our works but in virtue of his own purpose and the grace which he gave us in Christ Jesus ages ago, and now has manifested through the appearing of our Savior Christ Jesus, who abolished death and brought life and immortality to light through the gospel. (*II Timothy 1:8–10*)

Key Ideas: Strength to face suffering
Salvation is from God
Superiority over death

Action Step: Transform your daily work into a Christian vocation; find ways to be the best worker as a good Christian; when conditions are unbearable confront them boldly.

Prayer: Today, Lord, I believe I can share in the enrichment of Your world by faithfulness in my ordinary labor.

279 PERSONAL COMMITMENT

But I am not ashamed, for I know whom I have believed and I am sure that he is able to guard until that Day what has been entrusted to me. Follow the pattern of the sound words which you have heard from me, in the faith and love which are in Christ Jesus; guard the truth that has been entrusted to you by the Holy Spirit who dwells within us. *(II Timothy 1:12–14)*

Key Ideas: The ground of Christian confidence
Directives for Christian communication
The stewardship of the Gospel

Action Step: Challenge your church to become a guardian of the Gospel by supporting the work of one of the Bible translations and distribution societies.

Prayer: Lord, help me to keep true today to the faith You have given me in Yourself.

280 ENABLING TEACHERS

You then, my son, be strong in the grace that is in Christ Jesus, and what you have heard from me before many witnesses entrust to faithful men who will be able to teach others also. Share in suffering as a good soldier of Christ Jesus. No soldier on service gets entangled in civilian pursuits, since his aim is to satisfy the one who enlisted him. An athlete is not crowned unless he competes according to the rules. It is the hard-working farmer who ought to have the first share of the crops. *(II Timothy 2:1–6)*

Key Ideas: Commissioned for creative traditioning
Our allegiance as Christians
No substitute for hard work

Action Step: Patiently give of yourself to help new and inexperienced fellow Christians grow in some ability in Christian service or in some area of Christian knowledge.

Prayer: Stretch the muscles of my soul, Lord, and I will grow today.

281 A LONG-TERM COVENANT

The saying is sure:

> If we have died with him, we shall also live
>   with him;
> if we endure, we shall also reign with him;
> if we deny him, he also will deny us;
> if we are faithless, he remains faithful—

for he cannot deny himself. (*II Timothy 2:11–13*)

Key Ideas: The way of oneness with Christ
The victory is assured
The faithful Christ

Action Step: Visit an aging Christian friend; ask about some of his or her great life experiences.

Prayer: Knowing, Lord, that You will always be true to me challenges me today to want to stay true to You.

282 WORKERS UNASHAMED

Remind them of this, and charge them before the Lord to avoid disputing about words, which does no good, but only ruins the hearers. Do your best to present yourself to God as one approved, a workman who has no need to be ashamed, rightly handling the word of truth. (*II Timothy 2:14, 15*)

Key Ideas: Genuine dialogue that meets another
Learning to discern the Word of God
The highest accreditation of all

Action Step: Offer to assist another person to approach the Scripture in a spirit of fairness and honesty, setting aside biases that may result in twisting the Bible to his or her private interpretation.

Prayer: I am filled with thanksgiving today, Lord, for special persons who have taught me to love Your Scriptures and how to study them with integrity.

283 READY FOR ANY GOOD WORK

In a great house there are not only vessels of gold and silver but also of wood and earthenware, and some for noble use, some for ignoble. If any one purifies himself from what is ignoble, then he will be a vessel for noble use, consecrated and useful to the master of the house, ready for any good work. So shun youthful passions and aim at righteousness, faith, love, and peace, along with those who call upon the Lord from a pure heart. Have nothing to do with stupid, senseless controversies; you know that they breed quarrels. And the Lord's servant must not be quarrelsome but kindly to everyone, an apt teacher, forbearing, correcting his opponents with gentleness. God may perhaps grant that they will repent and come to know the truth, and they may escape from the snare of the devil, after being captured by him to do his will. (*II Timothy 2:20–26*)

Key Ideas: On call for the Master's use
The highway of Christian morality
A Christian style of communication

Action Step: Begin sharing your faith by offering to teach (or team teach) a children's, youth, or adult church class or group.

Prayer: Make me pure and good today, Lord, but pure and good for something instead of nothing.

284 INSPIRED SCRIPTURE FROM GOD

But as for you, continue in what you have learned and have firmly believed, knowing from whom you learned it and how from childhood you have been acquainted with the sacred writings which are able to instruct you for salvation through faith in Christ Jesus. All scripture is inspired by God and profitable for teaching, for reproof, for correction, and for training in righteousness, that the man of God may be complete, equipped for every good work. (*II Timothy 3:14–17*)

Key Ideas: Responding to our Christian heritage
A key source for Christian discipline
Readiness for Christian service

Action Step: Learn more about how our Bible came into being and how it has now become so available in most languages of our world.

Prayer: I am thrilled today, Lord, to know that I am a part of that great company of readers, teachers, translators, and distributors of the Bible throughout our world.

285 KEEPING THE FAITH

I charge you in the presence of God and of Christ Jesus who is to judge the living and the dead, and by his appearing and his kingdom: preach the word, be urgent in season and out of season, convince, rebuke, and exhort, be unfailing in patience and in teaching. For the time is coming when people will not endure sound teaching, but having itching ears they will accumulate for themselves teachers to suit their own likings, and will turn away from listening to the truth and wander into myths. As for you, always be steady, endure suffering, do the work of an evangelist, fulfil your ministry. For I am already on the point of being sacrificed; the time of my departure has come. I have fought the good fight, I have finished the race, I have kept the faith. Henceforth there is laid up for me the crown of righteousness, which the Lord, the righteous judge, will award to me on that Day, and not only to me but also to all who have loved his appearing. (*II Timothy 4:1–8*)

Key Ideas: Steady commitment to ministry
Hope made personal
The communion of the Saints

Action Step: Make a will or make sure your family and friends know your intentions about the legacy and belongings you will leave at death.

Prayer: Today, Lord, I'll keep my view on the far horizons.

286 MODELS FOR CHRIST

Show yourself in all respects a model of good deeds, and in your teaching show integrity, gravity, and sound speech that cannot be censured, so that an opponent may be put to shame, having nothing evil to say of us. Bid slaves to be submissive to their masters and to give satisfaction in every respect; they are not to be refractory, nor to pilfer, but to show entire and true fidelity, so that in everything they may adorn the doctrine of God our Savior. (*Titus 2:7–10*)

Key Ideas: Behavior that inspires
Communications that hold true
Witnessing that is indisputable

Action Step: Volunteer to work in a drama to be presented to or on behalf of your church.

Prayer: Lord, today let my life be a lens for Your light to shine through to others.

287 LIVING OUT OUR SALVATION

For the grace of God has appeared for the salvation of all men, training us to renounce irreligion and worldly passions, and to live sober, upright, and godly lives in this world, awaiting our blessed hope, the appearing of the glory of our great God and Savior Jesus Christ, who gave himself for us to redeem us from all iniquity and to purify for himself a people of his own who are zealous for good deeds. (*Titus 2:11–14*)

Key Ideas: Grace for holy living
Hope for our future
Sacrifice for salvation

Action Step: Translate your experience of salvation into a religion of holy actions.

Prayer: Lord, shake me up so that I may keep my total self in shape and always be ready for every opportunity to serve You today.

288 JUSTIFIED BY HIS GRACE

But when the goodness and loving kindness of God our Savior appeared, he saved us, not because of deeds done by us in righteousness, but in virtue of his own mercy, by the washing of regeneration and renewal in the Holy Spirit, which he poured out upon us richly through Jesus Christ our Savior, so that we might be justified by his grace and become heirs in hope of eternal life. (*Titus 3:4–7*)

Key Ideas: The advent of love in person
The recreative Holy Spirit
God's accepting love

Action Step: Decide how you may express God's kind of accepting love toward someone in trouble without appearing to approve of his or her misbehavior.

Prayer: Today, Lord, lead me toward right attitudes and acts of Christian generosity.

289 WORKING AND CARING

And let our people learn to apply themselves to good deeds, so as to help cases of urgent need, and not to be unfruitful. (*Titus 3:14*)

Key Ideas: Laboring at honorable occupations
Getting ourselves capable to care
A final test for faith

Action Step: Challenge a community or church group to commit itself to a project of rehabilitating the needy.

Prayer: Lord, I intend to honor You today in my daily work.

290 LOVE'S QUIET REVOLUTION

Accordingly, though I am bold enough in Christ to command you to do what is required, yet for love's sake I prefer to appeal to you—I, Paul, an ambassador and now a prisoner also for Christ Jesus—I appeal to you for my child, Onesimus, whose father I have become in my imprisonment. (Formerly he was useless to you, but now he is indeed useful to you and to me.) I am sending him back to you, sending my very heart. I would have been glad to keep him with me, in order that he might serve me on your behalf during my imprisonment for the gospel; but I preferred to do nothing without your consent in order that your goodness might not be by compulsion but of your own free will. Perhaps this is why he was parted from you for a while, that you might have him back forever, no longer as a slave but more than a slave, as a beloved brother, especially to me but how much more to you, both in the flesh and in the Lord. (*Philemon 8–16*)

Key Ideas: From alienation to reconciliation
A breakthrough against slavery
Using personal influence for Christ

Action Step: Move into some new area of human relationships using your personal influence for good.

Prayer: Lord, lead me today in challenging my friends in Christ's way.

291 HOW GOD SPEAKS

In many and various ways God spoke of old to our fathers by the prophets; but in these last days he has spoken to us by a Son, whom he appointed the heir of all things, through whom also he created the world. He reflects the glory of God and bears the very stamp of his nature, upholding the universe by his word of power. (*Hebrews 1:1–3*)

Key Ideas: The prophetic Word of God
The personal Word of God
The powerful Word of God

Action Step: Acquaint a friend with the various modern translations of the Bible; discover what Bible your church has on hand to share with children and inquiring adults.

Prayer: Basking in the sunshine of Your Word today, Lord, I will help scatter the Scriptures to hungering men, women, and children throughout the world.

292 DANGER IN NEGLECT

Therefore we must pay the closer attention to what we have heard, lest we drift away from it. For if the message declared by angels was valid and every transgression or disobedience received a just retribution, how shall we escape if we neglect such a great salvation? It was declared at first by the Lord, and it was attested to us by those who heard him, while God also bore witness by signs and wonders and various miracles and by gifts of the Holy Spirit distributed according to his own will. (*Hebrews 2:1–4*)

Key Ideas: Having so much that can be lost
The great salvation
Unforgettable works of God

Action Step: Take a personal inventory of your faith; ask yourself, "Is there some area of my Christian convictions and practice that is being neglected?"

Prayer: Lord, help me to keep up with my commitment today, because the last thing I want to do is to rust out as a Christian.

293 ONE WITH US

Since therefore the children share in flesh and blood, he himself likewise partook of the same nature, that through death he might destroy him who has the power of death, that is, the devil, and deliver all those who through fear of death were subject to lifelong bondage. For surely it is not with angels that he is concerned but with the descendants of Abraham. Therefore he had to be made like his brethren in every respect, so that he might become a merciful and faithful high priest in the service of God, to make expiation for the sins of the people. For because he himself has suffered and been tempted, he is able to help those who are tempted. (*Hebrews 2:14–18*)

Key Ideas: Christ's deliverance through death
Greatness through humiliation
He did something for all of us

Action Step: Once you have dealt with some frustrating phase of your spiritual development, enable someone else to make a breakthrough.

Prayer: Lord, I will walk today in the way Jesus Your Son has already traveled ahead of me.

294 AGAINST FALLING AWAY

Take care, brethren, lest there be in any of you an evil, unbelieving heart, leading you to fall away from the living God. But exhort one another every day, as long as it is called "today," that none of you may be hardened by the deceitfulness of sin. For we share in Christ, if only we hold our first confidence firm to the end. (*Hebrews 3:12–14*)

Key Ideas: The terrifying possibility of falling away
Staying spiritually alive each day
Keeping the faith all the way

Action Step: Be a "troublemaker" to a friend who needs you to stir him or her in continuing the struggle toward achieving a good and constructive life.

Prayer: Lord, I want to look carefully today how far I have allowed myself to drift away from Your fearful and inspiring presence.

295 GOD'S INCISIVE WORD

For the word of God is living and active, sharper than any two-edged sword, piercing to the division of soul and spirit, of joints and marrow, and discerning the thoughts and intentions of the heart. And before him no creature is hidden, but all are open and laid bare to the eyes of him with whom we have to do. (*Hebrews 4:12, 13*)

Key Ideas: God's penetrating Word
The heart has its reasons too
May as well be honest with God

Action Step: Invite a Christian psychiatrist or psychologist to your church to interpret—especially to the young people—the dynamics of personality, the inner self, conscience, and character.

Prayer: Even though it is a disturbing thought that You know me so intimately, Lord, nevertheless, I wish today to become more faithful to You.

296 CHRISTIAN CONFIDENCE

Since then we have a great high priest who has passed through the heavens, Jesus, the Son of God, let us hold fast our confession. For we have not a high priest who is unable to sympathize with our weaknesses, but one who in every respect has been tempted as we are, yet without sin. Let us then with confidence draw near to the throne of grace, that we may receive mercy and find grace to help in time of need. (*Hebrews 4:14–16*)

Key Ideas: Hold on to your faith
Jesus shows us how to hold on
God is able to uphold us

Action Step: Express openly and forthrightly your allegiance to Jesus as Lord who judges all human philosophies and systems; join with other Christians in public declaration of your faith.

Prayer: Lord, I will hold on to my faith today if You will fortify me with courage in spite of every human threat.

297 FOOD FOR GROWTH

For though by this time you ought to be teachers, you need some one to teach you again the first principles of God's word. You need milk, not solid food; for every one who lives on milk is unskilled in the word of righteousness, for he is a child. But solid food is for the mature, for those who have their faculties trained by practice to distinguish good from evil. (*Hebrews 5:12–14*)

Key Ideas: Potential to be teachers
Staying in kindergarten
Growing up in the faith

Action Step: Attend the next personal enrichment course planned by your church or the churches in your community; expand and deepen your understanding of the Christian faith, your communication skills, and your understanding of human nature.

Prayer: Fan the fire of my faith today, Lord, so that I may not be satisfied with spiritual mediocrity.

298 CONTINUING EDUCATION

Therefore let us leave the elementary doctrine of Christ and go on to maturity, not laying again a foundation of repentance from dead works and of faith toward God, with instruction about ablutions, the laying on of hands, the resurrection of the dead, and eternal judgment. And this we will do if God permits. For it is impossible to restore again to repentance those who have once been enlightened, who have tasted the heavenly gift, and have become partakers of the Holy Spirit, and have tasted the goodness of the word of God and the powers of the age to come, if they then commit apostasy, since they crucify the Son of God on their own account and hold him up to contempt. (*Hebrews 6:1–6*)

Key Ideas: The only way to grow
The point of no return
The crucifixion continues

Action Step: Give the price of a good book to your church, public, or college library.

Prayer: Lord, I cannot take lightly today the possibility that I could little by little move into an orbit of spiritual indifference to Your life-giving grace.

299 ANCHOR OF THE SOUL

So when God desired to show more convincingly to the heirs of the promise the unchangeable character of his purpose, he interposed with an oath, so that through two unchangeable things, in which it is impossible that God should prove false, we who have fled for refuge might have strong encouragement to seize the hope set before us. We have this as a sure and steadfast anchor of the soul, a hope that enters into the inner shrine behind the curtain, where Jesus has gone as a forerunner on our behalf, having become a high priest forever after the order of Melchizedek. (*Hebrews 6:17–20*)

Key Ideas: Our dependable God
Hope holds us sure
God of our future

Action Step: Memorize Psalm 23 or one of the great poems or hymns of assurance.

Prayer: Lord, help me to hang on to You today and not become unglued when pressures arise.

300 THE BLOOD OF CHRIST

For if sprinkling defiled persons with the blood of goats and bulls and with the ashes of a heifer sanctifies for the purification of the flesh, how much more shall the blood of Christ, who through the eternal Spirit offered himself without blemish to God, purify your conscience from dead works to serve the living God. (*Hebrews 9:13, 14*)

Key Ideas: Ancient ritual sacrifice
Christ's perfect offering to God
Cleansed for a life of service

Action Step: Expend *yourself*—not just money or token contributions—in one of the ministries or projects of your church; don't play games with Christ or your fellow Christians.

Prayer: The cost of Your persevering love, Lord, is a continual compulsion preventing me today from trying to take the cheap and easy way.

301 OUR GREAT HIGH PRIEST

For Christ has entered, not into a sanctuary made with hands, a copy of the true one, but into heaven itself, now to appear in the presence of God on our behalf. Nor was it to offer himself repeatedly, as the high priest enters the Holy Place yearly with blood not his own; for then he would have had to suffer repeatedly since the foundation of the world. But as it is, he has appeared once for all at the end of the age to put away sin by the sacrifice of himself. And just as it is appointed for men to die once, and after that comes judgment, so Christ, having been offered once to bear the sins of many, will appear a second time, not to deal with sin but to save those who are eagerly waiting for him. (*Hebrews 9:24–28*)

Key Ideas: The victory of Christ over death
The unique sacrifice of Christ
The hope of salvation with Christ

Action Step: Investigate the biographies of the leaders of the great world religions; compare them with Jesus; discover for yourself His superiority.

Prayer: Today I confidently face the challenges of my world and human existence because You, Lord, have made my forgiveness sure by the historical and spiritual sacrifice of Jesus the Christ.

302 THE NEW AND LIVING WAY

Therefore, brethren, since we have confidence to enter the sanctuary by the blood of Jesus, by the new and living way which he opened for us through the curtain, that is, through his flesh, and since we have a great priest over the house of God, let us draw near with a true heart in full assurance of faith, with our hearts sprinkled clean from an evil conscience and our bodies washed with pure water. Let us hold fast the confession of our hope without wavering, for he who promised is faithful; and let us consider how to stir up one another to love and good works, not neglecting to meet together, as is the habit of some, but encouraging one another, and all the more as you see the Day drawing near. (*Hebrews 10:19–25*)

Key Ideas: Our confidence in God's presence
Our confession of faith in Christ
Our community of concern in the Spirit

Action Step: Go to church worship next Sunday rejoicing in God; look for someone you may be able to encourage; be pleased with the sacrificial life of Christ regardless of the presentations of the choir, preacher, or anyone else.

Prayer: Lord, You have already accomplished through Your love in Jesus Christ so much beyond that which I can do today in gaining peaceful communion with You.

303 THE VISION OF FAITH

Now faith is the assurance of things hoped for, the conviction of things not seen. For by it the men of old received divine approval. By faith we understand that the world was created by the word of God, so that what is seen was made out of things which do not appear. (*Hebrews 11:1–3*)

Key Ideas: The certainty faith brings
The way to God's approval
Faith's understanding

Action Step: Say *yes* to the next daring and demanding assignment someone asks you to do; take a new leap of faith that will require total abandonment to trust in God.

Prayer: Lord, I am in great need today of some new venture that will stretch me beyond an overly cautious and calculated stance toward life.

304 THE ORIGIN OF FAITH

By faith Abraham obeyed when he was called to go out to a place which he was to receive as an inheritance; and he went out, not knowing where he was to go. By faith he sojourned in the land of promise, as in a foreign land, living in tents with Isaac and Jacob, heirs with him of the same promise. For he looked forward to the city which has foundations, whose builder and maker is God. (*Hebrews 11:8–10*)

Key Ideas: Abraham's invitation to adventure
Faith incorporates risk and responsibility
The heavenly goal of our earthly pilgrimage

Action Step: Risk doing that thing you have thought about—big or small—the outcome of which you are not sure, but which may force you to trust in God totally.

Prayer: Lord, enroll me today among Your pilgrim people.

305 THE GOAL OF GOD'S PEOPLE

These all died in faith, not having received what was promised, but having seen it and greeted it from afar, and having acknowledged that they were strangers and exiles on the earth. For people who speak thus make it clear that they are seeking a homeland. If they had been thinking of that land from which they had gone out, they would have had opportunity to return. But as it is, they desire a better country, that is, a heavenly one. Therefore God is not ashamed to be called their God, for he has prepared for them a city. (*Hebrews 11:13–16*)

Key Ideas: The vision of a promise
People on a pilgrimage
The heavenly city for God's people

Action Step: Honor one or all of God's saints who have served in centuries past by means of some act of loyalty to the principles for which they lived and died.

Prayer: Lord, keep me looking forward today even when I look back on the history of the people of faith.

306 JESUS OUR PIONEER

Therefore, since we are surrounded by so great a cloud of witnesses, let us also lay aside every weight, and sin which clings so closely, and let us run with perseverance the race that is set before us, looking to Jesus the pioneer and perfecter of our faith, who for the joy that was set before him endured the cross, despising the shame, and is seated at the right hand of the throne of God. (*Hebrews 12:1*, 2)

Key Ideas: Preparing for the race
Jesus our Pacesetter
The joy in the cross

Action Step: Begin each task of the day with a new commitment to finding the joy of Christian responsibility in it.

Prayer: Thank You, Lord, for today I am not alone because of Your gift of the communion of the saints.

307 THE REWARDS OF DISCIPLINE

God is treating you as sons; for what son is there whom his father does not discipline? If you are left without discipline, in which all have participated, then you are illegitimate children and not sons. Besides this, we have had earthly fathers to discipline us and we respected them. Shall we not much more be subject to the Father of spirits and live? For they disciplined us for a short time at their pleasure, but he disciplines us for our good, that we may share his holiness. For the moment all discipline seems painful rather than pleasant; later it yields the peaceful fruit of righteousness to those who have been trained by it. (*Hebrews 12:7–11*)

Key Ideas: The conditions of being God's children
The firmness of genuine love
The aim of God's disciplines

Action Step: Discuss with other parents how the disciplines of children can be carried out constructively with love.

Prayer: Lord, if today I must endure pain and suffering, I want to gain whatever wisdom is possible through the experience.

308 CHRIST FOR ALL SEASONS

Let brotherly love continue. Do not neglect to show hospitality to strangers, for thereby some have entertained angels unawares. Remember those who are in prison, as though in prison with them; and those who are ill-treated, since you also are in the body. Let marriage be held in honor among all, and let the marriage bed be undefiled; for God will judge the immoral and adulterous. Keep your life free from love of money, and be content with what you have; for he has said, "I will never fail you nor forsake you." Hence we can confidently say,

The Lord is my helper,
I will not be afraid;
what can man do to me?

Remember your leaders, those who spoke to you the word of God; consider the outcome of their life, and imitate their faith. Jesus Christ is the same yesterday and today and forever. Do not be led away by diverse and strange teachings; for it is well that the heart be strengthened by grace, not by foods, which have not benefited their adherents. (*Hebrews 13:1–9*)

Key Ideas: The outreaching compassionate life
The brightest lights of inspiration
Feeding on soul food

Action Step: Beginning in your own community enter into those compassionate activities that verify and embody the living presence of Jesus in our world today.

Prayer: Lord, keep my mind free today from willful prejudices that blind my best vision of others.

309 GOD'S NURTURING LOVE

Now may the God of peace who brought again from the dead our Lord Jesus, the great shepherd of the sheep, by the blood of the eternal covenant, equip you with everything good that you may do his will, working in you that which is pleasing in his sight, through Jesus Christ; to whom be glory for ever and ever. Amen. (*Hebrews 13:20, 21*)

Key Ideas: God's culmination of His covenant
God's continuing creation in us
God's goal for our life

Action Step: Join in some work project, ministry, or study program in which you may grow on the job and through dialogue with more experienced Christians.

Prayer: Lord, count me among those today who are willing to participate in the sacrificial life of Jesus.

310 THE WAY TO WISDOM

If any of you lacks wisdom, let him ask God who gives to all men generously and without reproaching, and it will be given him. But let him ask in faith, with no doubting, for he who doubts is like a wave of the sea that is driven and tossed by the wind. For that person must not suppose that a double-minded man, unstable in all his ways, will receive anything from the Lord. (*James 1:5–8*)

Key Ideas: The source of wisdom
The spirit of searching
The satisfactions of sincerity

Action Step: Take an idea, theory, or question and spend some time with it; first let it tumble around in your mind, then write down some notes, and follow up with some additional inquiries by reading, conversation, or testing it out.

Prayer: Lord, help me to keep at each task today even when I face a frustration over some obstacle in the way of mastery of a new problem or question.

311 EVERY GOOD GIFT

Blessed is the man who endures trial, for when he has stood the test he will receive the crown of life which God has promised to those who love him. Let no one say when he is tempted, "I am tempted by God"; for God cannot be tempted with evil and he himself tempts no one; but each person is tempted when he is lured and enticed by his own desire. Then desire when it has conceived gives birth to sin; and sin when it is full-grown brings forth death. Do not be deceived, my beloved brethren. Every good endowment and every perfect gift is from above, coming down from the Father of lights with whom there is no variation or shadow due to change. (*James 1:12–17*)

Key Ideas: True through the tests of life
God doesn't lead us into temptation
The radiating goodness of God

Action Step: Retravel one of the clear paths that your sanctified mind has shown you to be the way God is leading you out of temptation.

Prayer: I reach out to You today, Lord, for the life You are always giving with all its many-splendored joys and beauties.

312 HEARERS AND DOERS

Let every man be quick to hear, slow to speak, slow to anger, for the anger of man does not work the righteousness of God. Therefore put away all filthiness and rank growth of wickedness and receive with meekness the implanted word, which is able to save your souls. But be doers of the word, and not hearers only, deceiving yourselves. For if any one is a hearer of the word and not a doer, he is like a man who observes his natural face in a mirror; for he observes himself and goes away and at once forgets what he was like. But he who looks into the perfect law, the law of liberty, and perseveres, being no hearer that forgets but a doer that acts, he shall be blessed in his doing. (*James 1:19–25*)

Key Ideas: Keeping our communications cool
God's saving and stimulating word
Fulfillment in creative action

Action Step: Be alert to the things that too easily trigger from you irrational responses; don't fall for the bait others use to lure you into a fight with words, thoughts, or actions.

Prayer: Lord, give me insight into myself today when I think about the way I speak to my family, friends, and associates.

313 TRUE RELIGION

If any one thinks he is religious, and does not bridle his tongue but deceives his heart, this man's religion is vain. Religion that is pure and undefiled before God and the Father is this: to visit orphans and widows in their affliction, and to keep oneself unstained from the world. (*James 1:26*, 27)

Key Ideas: Religion of hollow thought
Religion of social responsibility
Religion of personal piety

Action Step: Visit a friend in the hospital and offer to be of assistance with special concerns.

Prayer: Lord, I will be bound to You today as I am bound to others in their need and to the inward growth of my own self.

314 BENEATH SURFACE APPEARANCES

My brethren, show no partiality as you hold the faith of our Lord Jesus Christ, the Lord of glory. For if a man with gold rings and in fine clothing comes into your assembly, and a poor man in shabby clothing also comes in, and you pay attention to the one who wears the fine clothing and say, "Have a seat here, please," while you say to the poor man, "Stand there," or, "Sit at my feet," have you not made distinctions among yourselves, and become judges with evil thoughts? Listen, my beloved brethren. Has not God chosen those who are poor in the world to be rich in faith and heirs of the kingdom which he has promised to those who love him? *(James 2:1–5)*

Key Ideas: Partiality is not Jesus' way
Kindness to every person
Another kind of wealth

Action Step: Be a personal ambassador for the Christ by helping persons feel welcome in your church regardless of their dress or external appearance.

Prayer: Lord, lead me today to love everyone I meet—even those whom I may not like.

315 THE LAW OF LIBERTY

If you really fulfil the royal law, according to the scripture, "You shall love your neighbor as yourself," you do well. But if you show partiality, you commit sin, and are convicted by the law as transgressors. For whoever keeps the whole law but fails in one point has become guilty of all of it. For he who said, "Do not commit adultery," said also, "Do not kill." If you do not commit adultery but do kill, you have become a transgressor of the law. So speak and so act as those who are to be judged under the law of liberty. For judgment is without mercy to one who has shown no mercy; mercy triumphs over judgment. *(James 2:8–13)*

Key Ideas: The heart of the Law
The problem of keeping the Law
The Law is never enough

Action Step: Bury the hatchet on a lingering grudge or resentment; move on to new freedom from the shackles of another's sin against you.

Prayer: What a relief I feel today, Lord, because You have shown me the need of forgiving others, starting with me.

316 FAITH AND WORKS

What does it profit, my brethren, if a man says he has faith but has not works? Can his faith save him? If a brother or sister is ill-clad and in lack of daily food, and one of you says to them, "Go in peace, be warmed and filled," without giving them the things needed for the body, what does it profit? So faith by itself, if it has no works, is dead. But some one will say, "You have faith and I have works." Show me your faith apart from your works, and I by my works will show you my faith. You believe that God is one; you do well. Even the demons believe—and shudder. Do you want to be shown, you shallow man, that faith apart from works is barren? Was not Abraham our father justified by works, when he offered his son Isaac upon the altar? You see that faith was active along with his works, and faith was completed by works, and the scripture was fulfilled which says, "Abraham believed God, and it was reckoned to him as righteousness"; and he was called the friend of God. You see that a man is justified by works and not by faith alone. (*James 2:14–24*)

Key Ideas: Faith versus works
Faith with works
The works of Abraham

Action Step: Think about something good you or your Christian fellowship have been promising to do; start the first steps now toward its completion.

Prayer: I know You are looking for evidences of my belief today, Lord, and I hope I may not disappoint You.

317 BLESSING AND CURSING

And the tongue is a fire. The tongue is an unrighteous world among our members, staining the whole body, setting on fire the cycle of nature, and set on fire by hell. For every kind of beast and bird, of reptile and sea creature, can be tamed and has been tamed by humankind, but no human being can tame the tongue—a restless evil, full of deadly poison. With it we bless the Lord and Father, and with it we curse men, who are made in the likeness of God. From the same mouth come blessing and cursing. (*James 3:6–10*)

Key Ideas: Dirty talk
Devil talk
Double talk

Action Step: Experiment in describing persons you don't like or with whom you are disgusted by omitting negative descriptive adjectives.

Prayer: Lord, when I whisper about someone today it will be a compliment.

318 SPIRITUAL WISDOM

Who is wise and understanding among you? By his good life let him show his works in the meekness of wisdom. But if you have bitter jealousy and selfish ambition in your hearts, do not boast and be false to the truth. This wisdom is not such as comes down from above, but is earthly, unspiritual, devilish. For where jealousy and selfish ambition exist, there will be disorder and every vile practice. But the wisdom from above is first pure, then peaceable, gentle, open to reason, full of mercy and good fruits, without uncertainty or insincerity. And the harvest of righteousness is sown in peace by those who make peace. (*James 3:13–18*)

Key Ideas: The meekness of wisdom
The masquerade of wisdom
The marks of wisdom

Action Step: Review and measure a recent learning or working experience by the Christian standard of wisdom.

Prayer: Lord, help me today to be patient with the pettiness and hang-ups of others.

319 MORE GRACE

Do you not know that friendship with the world is enmity with God? Therefore whoever wishes to be a friend of the world makes himself an enemy of God. Or do you suppose it is in vain that the scripture says, "He yearns jealously over the spirit which he has made to dwell in us"? But he gives more grace; therefore it says, "God opposes the proud, but gives grace to the humble." Submit yourselves therefore to God. Resist the devil and he will flee from you. Draw near to God and he will draw near to you. (*James 4:4–8*)

Key Ideas: The highest friendship
When God can help us
How to beat the devil

Action Step: Turn away from those activities and interests that trouble your conscience; turn toward pursuits in which you can be glad about God's presence.

Prayer: When I act less than my best self today, Lord, shake me up with whatever is necessary to turn me closer to You.

320 TENTATIVE TOMORROWS

Come now, you who say, "Today or tomorrow we will go into such and such a town and spend a year there and trade and get gain"; whereas you do not know about tomorrow. What is your life? For you are a mist that appears for a little time and then vanishes. Instead you ought to say, "If the Lord wills, we shall live and we shall do this or that." As it is, you boast in your arrogance. All such boasting is evil. Whoever knows what is right to do and fails to do it, for him it is sin. (*James 4:13–17*)

Key Ideas: Warning to the confident
Reservations about tomorrow
When in doubt be positive

Action Step: If you are bewildered about a major decision for your future, move forward one step at a time with what you know you should do now; your alternatives may gradually appear on the horizon.

Prayer: Lord, keep me within the speed limit of Your Spirit today.

321 JUDGMENT ON INJUSTICE

Behold, the wages of the laborers who mowed your fields, which you kept back by fraud, cry out; and the cries of the harvesters have reached the ears of the Lord of hosts. You have lived on the earth in luxury and in pleasure; you have fattened your hearts in a day of slaughter. You have condemned, you have killed the righteous man; he does not resist you. (*James 5:4–6*)

Key Ideas: Economic injustice
Misuse of affluence
Reliance on violence

Action Step: Examine the selfish and unjust demands you or your associates are making on others; determine to make the changes you can before it is too late for them and you.

Prayer: Lord, when I am indicted today by Your penetrating truth I want to run, but there is no hiding place.

322 THE POWER OF PRAYER

Is any one among you suffering? Let him pray. Is any cheerful? Let him sing praise. Is any among you sick? Let him call for the elders of the church, and let them pray over him, anointing him with oil in the name of the Lord; and the prayer of faith will save the sick man, and the Lord will raise him up; and if he has committed sins, he will be forgiven. Therefore confess your sins to one another, and pray for one another, that you may be healed. The prayer of a righteous man has great power in its effects. *(James 5:13–16)*

Key Ideas: The healing Christian fellowship
Priests to one another
Tremendous power in prayer

Action Step: Make a prayer list of persons within your various spheres of acquaintance and association.

Prayer: Teach me more today, Lord, about the ministry of prayer for and with others.

323 BRING THEM BACK

My brethren, if any one among you wanders from the truth and some one brings him back, let him know that whoever brings back a sinner from the error of his way will save his soul from death and will cover a multitude of sins. *(James 5:19, 20)*

Key Ideas: Truth is a way of living
Our Christian rescue mission
Deliverance from the deadening past

Action Step: Find a friend who has dropped out of the church and gently lead him or her back into a life-nurturing fellowship.

Prayer: Your forgiving grace, Lord, gives me new purpose for living for others today.

324 A LIVING HOPE

Blessed be the God and Father of our Lord Jesus Christ! By his great mercy we have been born anew to a living hope through the resurrection of Jesus Christ from the dead, and to an inheritance which is imperishable, undefiled, and unfading, kept in heaven for you, who by God's power are guarded through faith for a salvation ready to be revealed in the last time. In this you rejoice, though now for a little while you may have to suffer various trials, so that the genuineness of your faith, more precious than gold which though perishable is tested by fire, may redound to praise and glory and honor at the revelation of Jesus Christ. Without having seen him you love him; though you do not now see him you believe in him and rejoice with unutterable and exalted joy. As the outcome of your faith you obtain the salvation of your souls. (*I Peter 1:3–9*)

Key Ideas: The new birth of hope in Christ
Our glorious destiny
A faith that can be tested

Action Step: Prove the sincerity and seriousness of your commitment to Christ; take the initiative in expressing your deep trust in Christ to someone doubting the relevance of Christ to our world.

Prayer: Even though I may tremble, Lord, lead me today to do some quiet courageous witnessing for the Christ.

325 A HOLY LIFE

Therefore gird up your minds, be sober, set your hope fully upon the grace that is coming to you at the revelation of Jesus Christ. As obedient children, do not be conformed to the passions of your former ignorance, but as he who called you is holy, be holy yourselves in all your conduct; since it is written, "You shall be holy, for I am holy." (*I Peter 1:13–16*)

Key Ideas: Be sober
Be obedient
Be holy

Action Step: Shape for yourself a workable pattern of spiritual discipline for your personal enrichment and equipment for Christian ministry and witness.

Prayer: Lord, I hope to experience today the power of personal obedience to the way of Christ.

326 LIVING STONES

So put away all malice and all guile and insincerity and envy and all slander. Like newborn babes, long for the pure spiritual milk, that by it you may grow up to salvation; for you have tasted the kindness of the Lord. Come to him, to that living stone, rejected by men but in God's sight chosen and precious; and like living stones be yourselves built into a spiritual house, to be a holy priesthood, to offer spiritual sacrifices acceptable to God through Jesus Christ. (*I Peter 2:1–5*)

Key Ideas: Salvation is a growth process
God's building of new relationships
A priestly ministry for all persons

Action Step: Decide on one person in your Christian fellowship whom you can especially encourage; seek to inspire him or her in greater growth with an invitation to a small-group learning event.

Prayer: Let my work today, Lord, be an expression of my spiritual service to You.

327 CHOSEN FOR MISSION

But you are a chosen race, a royal priesthood, a holy nation, God's own people, that you may declare the wonderful deeds of him who called you out of darkness into his marvelous light. Once you were no people but now you are God's people; once you had not received mercy but now you have received mercy. (*I Peter 2:9, 10*)

Key Ideas: A special position for mission
Announcing the mighty deeds of God
A new creation from God

Action Step: Make a chart or diagram showing the many ways members of your church move out as a witnessing people of God into community service and organizations.

Prayer: Lord, since You have called me to be a part of Your chosen people, I will today accept this high opportunity to bear the light of Your love to the whole world.

328 FREEDOM UNDER GOD

Be subject for the Lord's sake to every human institution, whether it be to the emperor as supreme, or to governors as sent by him to punish those who do wrong and to praise those who do right. For it is God's will that by doing right you should put to silence the ignorance of foolish men. Live as free men, yet without using your freedom as a pretext for evil; but live as servants of God. Honor all men. Love the brotherhood. Fear God. Honor the emperor. (*I Peter 2:13–17*)

Key Ideas: Good governments are servants of God
Attacking criticism with positive action
Freedom is for living a life of service

Action Step: Join a political party or organization with the purpose of keeping it more responsive to the cause of justice and constructive legislation.

Prayer: Lord, help me to be as eager today to promote the rights and freedoms of others as for myself.

329 IN HIS STEPS

For to this you have been called, because Christ also suffered for you, leaving you an example, that you should follow in his steps. He committed no sin; no guile was found on his lips. When he was reviled, he did not revile in return; when he suffered, he did not threaten; but he trusted to him who judges justly. He himself bore our sins in his body on the tree, that we might die to sin and live to righteousness. By his wounds you have been healed. For you were straying like sheep, but have now returned to the Shepherd and Guardian of your souls. (*I Peter 2:21–25*)

Key Ideas: Christ's way is our way too
The victory of nonviolence
Christ's life was offered for us

Action Step: Look at a major role you have accepted—parent, partner, member, or leader—and ask yourself, "How in this relationship can I walk in His steps?"

Prayer: Lord, by Your inspiration of my mind today, I will translate the cross of Jesus into personal responsibility.

330 DEFENDING OUR FAITH

Now who is there to harm you if you are zealous for what is right? But even if you do suffer for righteousness' sake, you will be blessed. Have no fear of them, nor be troubled, but in your hearts reverence Christ as Lord. Always be prepared to make a defense to any one who calls you to account for the hope that is in you, yet do it with gentleness and reverence; and keep your conscience clear, so that, when you are abused, those who revile your good behavior in Christ may be put to shame. For it is better to suffer for doing right, if that should be God's will, then for doing wrong. (*I Peter 3:13–17*)

Key Ideas: Reverence for Christ above all
Ready to respond with hope
The highest kind of persuasion

Action Step: Among Christian friends review your own personal story—how the Christian faith has touched the depth of your being—in order to be able and ready to explain your faith wisely to non-Christians.

Prayer: Lord, I will work today to earn the right to be heard by others—by living the Gospel before I demand that they listen to my Good News.

331 LOVE COVERS SINS

Above all hold unfailing your love for one another, since love covers a multitude of sins. Practice hospitality ungrudgingly to one another. As each has received a gift, employ it for one another, as good stewards of God's varied grace: whoever speaks, as one who utters oracles of God; whoever renders service, as one who renders it by the strength which God supplies; in order that in every thing God may be glorified through Jesus Christ. To him belong glory and dominion for ever and ever. Amen. (*I Peter 4:8–11*)

Key Ideas: The healing quality of love
Gifts and talents for sharing
The chief goal of a Christian: praise to God

Action Step: Make another effort or gesture of understanding toward someone who has felt hurt or damaged by you or by a group with whom you are associated.

Prayer: Today, Lord, if You will excuse some natural hesitancy I will try to develop a talent or skill other than my usual strengths.

332 CHRISTIAN UNASHAMED

Beloved, do not be surprised at the fiery ordeal which comes upon you to prove you, as though something strange were happening to you. But rejoice in so far as you share Christ's sufferings, that you may also rejoice and be glad when his glory is revealed. If you are reproached for the name of Christ, you are blessed, because the spirit of glory and of God rests upon you. But let none of you suffer as a murderer, or a thief, or a wrongdoer, or a mischief-maker; yet if one suffers as a Christian, let him not be ashamed, but under that name let him glorify God. (*I Peter 4:12–16*)

Key Ideas: Troubles because we are with Christ
Some suffering is not God's will
Life that honors God

Action Step: Become informed about the present sufferings and imprisonments of Christians around the world; join with others in prayer, protest, and measures to secure justice and their freedom.

Prayer: Lord, if today or some day I am called to suffer because of my Christian convictions, I want to be a worthy witness of the Christ.

333 GOD'S CARING

Humble yourselves therefore under the mighty hand of God, that in due time he may exalt you. Cast all your anxieties on him, for he cares about you. Be sober, be watchful. Your adversary the devil prowls around like a roaring lion, seeking someone to devour. Resist him, firm in your faith, knowing that the same experience of suffering is required of your brotherhood throughout the world. (*I Peter 5:6–9*)

Key Ideas: Learning to trust in God
Awake for your soul's sake
The brotherhood of suffering

Action Step: Make a list of your major worries and anxieties; then ask God's guidance in dealing with them or discarding them from your mind's preoccupation.

Prayer: Lord, I know You have the whole world in Your hands today, but I do have a persistent problem of presuming that this includes everyone's cares but mine.

334 A BALANCED LIFE

For this very reason make every effort to supplement your faith with virtue, and virtue with knowledge, and knowledge with self-control, and self-control with steadfastness, and steadfastness with godliness, and godliness with brotherly affection, and brotherly affection with love. For if these things are yours and abound, they keep you from being ineffective or unfruitful in the knowledge of our Lord Jesus Christ. For whoever lacks these things is blind and shortsighted and has forgotten that he was cleansed from his old sins. Therefore, brethren, be the more zealous to confirm your call and election, for if you do this you will never fall; so there will be richly provided for you an entrance into the eternal kingdom of our Lord and Savior Jesus Christ. (*II Peter 1:5–11*)

Key Ideas: The chain of Christian growth
Equipped for ministry and witness
God's choice and our choice

Action Step: Take up the disciplines of Christian discipleship at this stage of your life and spiritual pilgrimage which can present additional occasions for personal growth.

Prayer: I want to chew on some spiritual proteins today, Lord, in place of only the sweets of the Spirit.

335 AGAINST TURNING BACK

For if, after they have escaped the defilements of the world through the knowledge of our Lord and Savior Jesus Christ, they are again entangled in them and overpowered, the last state has become worse for them than the first. For it would have been better for them never to have known the way of righteousness than after knowing it to turn back from the holy commandment delivered to them. It has happened to them according to the true proverb, The dog turns back to his own vomit, and the sow is washed only to wallow in the mire. (*II Peter 2:20–22*)

Key Ideas: Salvation can be lost
Sin in slighting God's commandments
Spiritual defection—a sad condition

Action Step: Construct a mental picture of yourself in a healthy spiritual condition having overcome one or two of your major sins.

Prayer: Lord, keep me alert today to the forces that build up and tear down my spiritual well-being.

336 GOD'S TIME AND OURS

But do not ignore this one fact, beloved, that with the Lord one day is as a thousand years, and a thousand years as one day. The Lord is not slow about his promise as some count slowness, but is forbearing toward you, not wishing that any should perish, but that all should reach repentance. But the day of the Lord will come like a thief, and then the heavens will pass away with a loud noise, and the elements will be dissolved with fire, and the earth and the works that are upon it will be burned up. Since all these things are thus to be dissolved, what sort of persons ought you to be in lives of holiness and godliness, waiting for and hastening the coming of the day of God. (*II Peter 3:8–12*)

Key Ideas: The patient love of God
The inevitable judgment of God
The inspiring holiness of God

Action Step: In your conversation with a friend, express your concern for the choice opportunities each new day offers.

Prayer: Lord, today I will measure my life by its quality even when I can't be sure of its length.

337 FIRST-HAND FAITH

That which was from the beginning, which we have heard, which we have seen with our eyes, which we have looked upon and touched with our hands, concerning the word of life—the life was made manifest, and we saw it, and testify to it, and proclaim to you the eternal life which was with the Father and was made manifest to us—that which we have seen and heard we proclaim also to you, so that you may have fellowship with us; and our fellowship is with the Father and with his Son Jesus Christ. (*I John 1:1–3*)

Key Ideas: The faith of experience
The faith we proclaim
The fellowship of faith

Action Step: Risk talking about your beliefs, describing in your own words how Jesus is a living Presence within you.

Prayer: Today, Lord, I will try to convince others about my faith, especially when I have first-hand experience.

338 GUILT IS REAL

If we confess our sins, he is faithful and just, and will forgive our sins and cleanse us from all unrighteousness. If we say we have not sinned, we make him a liar, and his word is not in us. My little children, I am writing this to you so that you may not sin; but if any one does sin, we have an advocate with the Father, Jesus Christ the righteous; and he is the expiation for our sins, and not for ours only but also for the sins of the whole world. (*I John 1:9–2:2*)

Key Ideas: Facing up to our sins
Seeking to avoid sin
Christ's offering for our sins

Action Step: Help someone discover the Church as a fellowship of forgiven sinners and struggling saints.

Prayer: Lord, I am overwhelmed with thanksgiving today for such forgiving love that includes me as well as the whole world.

339 THIS WORLD'S LIMITATIONS

Do not love the world or the things in the world. If any one loves the world, love for the Father is not in him. For all that is in the world, the lust of the flesh and the lust of the eyes and the pride of life, is not of the Father but is of the world. And the world passes away, and the lust of it; but he who does the will of God abides forever. (*I John 2:15–17*)

Key Ideas: Misplaced loyalty
Negative side of the world
Finding that which endures

Action Step: Examine your way of looking at persons, things, and opportunities; ask yourself, "What new life could open before me if I looked at the world unselfishly, unpossessively, humbly?"

Prayer: Lord, help me to put all the good as well as the bad "things" in their proper perspective so that I may begin even today that life with You that endures forever.

340 CHILDREN OF GOD

See what love the Father has given us, that we should be called children of God; and so we are. The reason why the world does not know us is that it did not know him. Beloved, we are God's children now; it does not yet appear what we shall be, but we know that when he appears we shall be like him, for we shall see him as he is. And every one who thus hopes in him purifies himself as he is pure. (*I John 3:1–3*)

Key Ideas: The gift of basic identity
Our growing communion with Christ
The pull of high aspirations

Action Step: Find some occasion to affirm to another who you really are because of your relationship to God.

Prayer: Lord, knowing I am Your child today brings me a new awareness of strength and freedom.

341 THE ART OF LOVING

We know that we have passed out of death into life, because we love the brethren. He who does not love abides in death. Any one who hates his brother is a murderer, and you know that no murderer has eternal life abiding in him. By this we know love, that he laid down his life for us; and we ought to lay down our lives for the brethren. But if any one has the world's goods and sees his brother in need, yet closes his heart against him, how does God's love abide in him? Little children, let us not love in word or speech but in deed and in truth. (*I John 3:14–18*)

Key Ideas: The new birth of love
The final proof of love
The practical way of love

Action Step: Consider which service or action projects in your community are worthy of your support by money and personal talent.

Prayer: Lord, I am ready today to work to free the streams of love in our world from the pollution of selfishness and greed.

342 GOD IS GREATER

By this we shall know that we are of the truth, and reassure our hearts before him whenever our hearts condemn us; for God is greater than our hearts, and he knows everything. Beloved, if our hearts do not condemn us, we have confidence before God; and we receive from him whatever we ask, because we keep his commandments and do what pleases him. (*I John 3:19–22*)

Key Ideas: When God must uphold us
When we can feel bold
When prayer works

Action Step: Help a downcast brother or sister to discover and affirm that God loves us even when we don't always think or feel we are good.

Prayer: Lord, today I simply want to gain strength from an awareness of Your greatness that reaches beyond the farthest reach of my mind and heart.

343 CHRISTIAN LOYALTY

Beloved, do not believe every spirit, but test the spirits to see whether they are of God; for many false prophets have gone out into the world. By this you know the Spirit of God: every spirit which confesses that Jesus Christ has come in the flesh is of God, and every spirit which does not confess Jesus is not of God. This is the spirit of antichrist, of which you heard that it was coming, and now it is in the world already. (*I John 4:1–3*)

Key Ideas: Skepticism over the prophets
The Holy Spirit empowers the prophets
The central creed of the Christian

Action Step: Verify the reliability, accountability, and affiliations of religious broadcasts and fund raisers who seek your theological agreement and financial support.

Prayer: Show me how to be fair in my judging of others today, Lord, while I assume my responsibility of holding true to the heart of Christianity.

344 GOD'S CREATIVE LOVE

Beloved, let us love one another; for love is of God, and he who loves is born of God and knows God. He who does not love does not know God; for God is love. In this the love of God was made manifest among us, that God sent his only Son into the world, so that we might live through him. In this is love, not that we love God but that he loved us and sent his Son to be the expiation for our sins. (*I John 4:7–10*)

Key Ideas: Born into love
Our model of love
Genesis of sacrificial love

Action Step: Translate your love for God into the currency of human brotherhood exchangeable in the local community in which you are now living.

Prayer: Lord, I am humbled and happy today knowing that as a Christian I am capable of being an instrument of Your love for others.

345 LOVE CONQUERS FEAR

Whoever confesses that Jesus is the Son of God, God abides in him, and he in God. So we know and believe the love God has for us. God is love, and he who abides in love abides in God, and God abides in him. In this is love perfected with us, that we may have confidence for the day of judgment, because as he is so are we in this world. There is no fear in love, but perfect love casts out fear. For fear has to do with punishment, and he who fears is not perfected in love. We love, because he first loved us. *(I John 4:15–19)*

Key Ideas: The Christ defines God's love
The deliverance love brings
The source of true love

Action Step: Walk cheerfully wherever you go as one who knows what it means to be loved and forgiven by God's perfect love.

Prayer: Today, Lord, I intend to live with a calm confidence in Your sovereign love.

346 VICTORY THROUGH FAITH

Every one who believes that Jesus is the Christ is a child of God, and every one who loves the parent loves the child. By this we know that we love the children of God, when we love God and obey his commandments. For this is the love of God, that we keep his commandments. And his commandments are not burdensome. For whatever is born of God overcomes the world; and this is the victory that overcomes the world, our faith. Who is it that overcomes the world but he who believes that Jesus is the Son of God? *(I John 5:1–5)*

Key Ideas: Children of God by faith
Ungrudging obedience to God
With God we shall overcome

Action Step: Begin to treat persons regardless of their apparent high or low status with respect as children of God; believe in them as you wish them to behave toward you.

Prayer: Lord, since I am inclined with my temptations to play the "victim"; let me live today as one who is overcoming what I can and enduring in a Christlike manner what I can't change.

347 LOOKING AHEAD

Look to yourselves, that you may not lose what you have worked for, but may win a full reward. (*II John 8*)

Key Ideas: Beginning within
Losing our treasure
Aiming high

Action Step: Take care of yourself spiritually; give your soul a beauty treatment.

Prayer: Lord, I am going to stay alert today and keep growing toward Your Kingdom's goal.

348 THINKING OF OTHERS

Beloved, I pray that all may go well with you and that you may be in health; I know it is well with your soul. (*III John 2*)

Key Ideas: Wishing others well
Our physical fitness responsibility
Keeping our soul healthy too

Action Step: Make an appointment to have a physical checkup if it has been some time since you have seen a doctor.

Prayer: Slow me down today, Lord, in order that I may better sense my own physical condition.

349 DOING GOOD

Beloved, do not imitate evil but imitate good. He who does good is of God; he who does evil has not seen God. (*III John 11*)

Key Ideas: Conformity with excellence
The Source of our goodness
The proof of denying God

Action Step: Reflect on the spirit and style of a living Christian saint whom you know, and, while staying your natural self, try to do some Christian act the way that saint would go about it.

Prayer: Sharpen my conscience today, Lord, in order that I may determine more clearly the difference between good and evil.

350 FAITH TO SHARE

But you, beloved, build yourselves up on your most holy faith; pray in the Holy Spirit; keep yourselves in the love of God; wait for the mercy of our Lord Jesus Christ unto eternal life. And convince some, who doubt; save some, by snatching them out of the fire; on some have mercy with fear, hating even the garment spotted by the flesh. (*Jude 20–23*)

Key Ideas: Work on yourself first
Keep the long view of hope
A threefold rescue mission

Action Step: Meet with other Christians and compare positive and negative experiences you have had in helping persons in the Christian way.

Prayer: Lord, I know I need Your forgiveness for myself today, even while I encourage others to seek forgiveness for themselves.

351 HELP FROM FALLING

Now to him who is able to keep you from falling and to present you without blemish before the presence of his glory with rejoicing, to the only God, our Savior through Jesus Christ our Lord, be glory, majesty, dominion, and authority, before all time and now and forever. Amen. (*Jude 24, 25*)

Key Ideas: With God's help we can stand
In God's company without fear
Our eternal God and Christ

Action Step: Ask yourself, "Are there any areas of my life in which I presume I can shift my own scale of values and not slip far off the right track?"

Prayer: Dear Lord, help me today not to stumble over my own feet.

352 ALPHA AND OMEGA

To him who loves us and has freed us from our sins by his blood and made us a kingdom, priests to his God and Father, to him be glory and dominion for ever and ever. Amen. Behold, he is coming with the clouds, and every eye will see him, every one who pierced him; and all tribes of the earth will wail on account of him. Even so. Amen. "I am the Alpha and the Omega," says the Lord God, who is and who was and who is to come, the Almighty. (*Revelation 1:5–8*)

Key Ideas: Loved, liberated, and commissioned
The universal recognition of the Christ
God's eternal being and becoming

Action Step: Work on establishing credentials of Christian character and spirit as well as education, experience, and expertise.

Prayer: I live in Your love today, Lord, and feel I am being drawn—throughout my whole lifetime—into a sacrificial life with Jesus my Christ.

353 CALL TO FAITHFULNESS

I know your tribulation and your poverty (but you are rich) and the slander of those who say that they are Jews and are not, but are a synagogue of Satan. Do not fear what you are about to suffer. Behold, the devil is about to throw some of you into prison, that you may be tested, and for ten days you will have tribulation. Be faithful unto death, and I will give you the crown of life. He who has an ear, let him hear what the Spirit says to the churches. He who conquers shall not be hurt by the second death. (*Revelation 2:9–11*)

Key Ideas: When people underestimate us
The devil never lets up
Royal rewards await the faithful

Action Step: Refuse to be intimidated or go along with anyone who acts like the devil; oppose evil all around you.

Prayer: I surely will not be stifled by the subtleties of Satan today, Lord, since I can be guided by wisdom and courage from You.

354 THE WELCOME DOOR

I know your works; you are neither cold nor hot. Would that you were cold or hot! So, because you are lukewarm, and neither cold nor hot, I will spew you out of my mouth. For you say, I am rich, I have prospered, and I need nothing; not knowing that you are wretched, pitiable, poor, blind and naked. Therefore I counsel you to buy from me gold refined by fire, that you may be rich, and white garments to clothe you and to keep the shame of your nakedness from being seen, and salve to anoint your eyes, that you may see. Those whom I love, I reprove and chasten; so be zealous and repent. Behold, I stand at the door and knock; if any one hears my voice and opens the door, I will come in to him and eat with him, and he with me. (*Revelation 3:15–20*)

Key Ideas: Indictment of spiritual smugness
Suggestions for spiritual renewal
Christ always standing at the door

Action Step: If it is true, then face up to the mediocrity, poverty, or sickness of your soul; start the struggle again for the refreshing life of repentance in Christ's way.

Prayer: Help me, Lord, to be tuned in to what Your Spirit is saying to the churches today.

355 THE PRAISE OF MANY

After this I looked, and behold, a great multitude which no man could number, from every nation, from all tribes and peoples and tongues, standing before the throne and before the Lamb, clothed in white robes, with palm branches in their hands, and crying out with a loud voice, "Salvation belongs to our God who sits upon the throne, and to the Lamb!" And all the angels stood round the throne and round the elders and the four living creatures, and they fell on their faces before the throne and worshiped God, saying, "Amen! Blessing and glory and wisdom and thanksgiving and honor and power and might be to our God for ever and ever! Amen." (*Revelation 7:9–12*)

Key Ideas: The vision of a large heaven
The mystery of mercy and might
The highest form of prayer

Action Step: Make your thoughts and feelings known on the necessity of having a genuine "all people's church" in your community.

Prayer: Lord, I feel the surge today of new strength in knowing I am called as a Christian into a world fellowship of Christians.

356 PRAYERS OF THE SAINTS

When the Lamb opened the seventh seal, there was silence in heaven for about half an hour. Then I saw the seven angels who stand before God, and seven trumpets were given to them. And another angel came and stood at the altar with a golden censer; and he was given much incense to mingle with the prayers of all the saints upon the golden altar before the throne; and the smoke of the incense rose with the prayers of the saints from the hand of the angel before God. Then the angel took the censer and filled it with fire from the altar and threw it on the earth; and there were peals of thunder, loud voices, flashes of lightning, and an earthquake. (*Revelation 8:1–5*)

Key Ideas: The messengers of God
The Church at prayer
Our prayers are part of God's purpose

Action Step: Enter into a continuing covenant of prayer with other Christians, of communion with God, and of compassionate Christian action.

Prayer: Lord, expand my awareness today of the total dimensions of prayer that fully participates in Your activity in the world.

357 THE SWEET AND BITTER

Then the voice which I had heard from heaven spoke to me again, saying, "Go, take the scroll which is open in the hand of the angel who is standing on the sea and on the land." So I went to the angel and told him to give me the little scroll; and he said to me, "Take it and eat; it will be bitter to your stomach, but sweet as honey in your mouth." And I took the little scroll from the hand of the angel and ate it; it was sweet as honey in my mouth, but when I had eaten it my stomach was made bitter. And I was told, "You must again prophesy about many peoples and nations and tongues and kings." (*Revelation 10:8–11*)

Key Ideas: In company with spiritual powers
The dual direction of the Word
Assuming the prophetic task

Action Step: Commit yourself to follow the logical argument of a book, magazine, paper, or media program dealing with a contemporary public concern even if it has a disturbing message.

Prayer: Lord, the truth is what I need today, even if a half truth is what I prefer to hear.

358 THE KINGDOM FOREVER

Then the seventh angel blew his trumpet, and there were loud voices in heaven, saying, "The kingdom of the world has become the kingdom of our Lord and of his Christ, and he shall reign for ever and ever." And the twenty-four elders who sit on their thrones before God fell on their faces and worshiped God, saying,

> We give thanks to thee, Lord God Almighty, who art and who wast, that thou hast taken thy great power and begun to reign. The nations raged, but thy wrath came, and the time for the dead to be judged, for rewarding thy servants, the prophets and saints, and those who fear thy name, both small and great, and for destroying the destroyers of the earth.

(*Revelation 11:15–18*)

Key Ideas: Our world restored
Our eternal God
Our history has a goal

Action Step: Attempt to express in poetry, painting, music, or other artistic medium that which affirms with confidence God's rule over our universe.

Prayer: I will find hope no matter what today holds for me, Lord, for Your promises are trustworthy above all.

359 END OF ALL EVIL

Now war arose in heaven, Michael and his angels fighting against the dragon; and the dragon and his angels fought, but they were defeated and there was no longer any place for them in heaven. And the great dragon was thrown down, that ancient serpent, who is called the Devil and Satan, the deceiver of the whole world—he was thrown down to the earth, and his angels were thrown down with him. And I heard a loud voice in heaven, saying, "Now the salvation and the power and the kingdom of our God and the authority of his Christ have come, for the accuser of our brethren has been thrown down, who accuses them day and night before our God. And they have conquered him by the blood of the Lamb and by the word of their testimony, for they loved not their lives even unto death." (*Revelation 12:7–11*)

Key Ideas: The great accomplishment
The defeat of the devil
The saints share the victory

Action Step: Participate in a dialogue with a group of Christian friends concerning the crucial beliefs that a Christian must be willing to suffer for if it is ever required.

Prayer: I will find new strength for witnessing today, Lord, knowing the victory is assured.

360 EVERLASTING REST

Here is a call for the endurance of the saints, those who keep the commandments of God and the faith of Jesus. And I heard a voice from heaven saying, "Write this: Blessed are the dead who die in the Lord henceforth." "Blessed indeed," says the Spirit, "that they may rest from their labors, for their deeds follow them!" (*Revelation 14:12, 13*)

Key Ideas: The length of commitment
Standing with Christ against evil
If we give our all

Action Step: Contribute some of your time, talents, and money to a cause or the church in combating a destructive activity in our society.

Prayer: Courage, Lord, is what I need to keep true to the right today.

361 GOD OF THE UNIVERSE

And I saw what appeared to be a sea of glass mingled with fire, and those who had conquered the beast and its image and the number of its name, standing beside the sea of glass with harps of God in their hands. And they sing the song of Moses, the servant of God, and the song of the Lamb, saying,

> Great and wonderful are thy deeds,
> O Lord God the Almighty!
> Just and true are thy ways,
> O King of the ages!
> Who shall not fear and glorify thy name, O Lord?
> For thou alone art holy.
> All nations shall come and worship thee,
> for thy judgments have been revealed.

(Revelation 15:2–4)

Key Ideas: A song of deliverance and redemption
The faithfulness of God
God over all

Action Step: Tell someone of your experience of freedom of the Spirit and its satisfactions in addition to the civil rights and political freedoms you enjoy or long for.

Prayer: Lord, I will live as a free person today because You rule the universe.

362 THE TRIUMPHANT WORD

Then I saw heaven opened, and behold, a white horse! He who sat upon it is called Faithful and True, and in righteousness he judges and makes war. His eyes are like a flame of fire, and on his head are many diadems; and he has a name inscribed which no one knows but himself. He is clad in a robe dipped in blood, and the name by which he is called is The Word of God. And the armies of heaven, arrayed in fine linen, white and pure, followed him on white horses. From his mouth issues a sharp sword with which to smite the nations, and he will rule them with a rod of iron; he will tread the wine press of the fury of the wrath of God the Almighty. On his robe and on his thigh he has a name inscribed, King of kings and Lord of lords. *(Revelation 19:11–16)*

Key Ideas: Warfare of the Spirit
Wardrobe of the soldiers
Weapons of the warrior

Action Step: Consider in what areas of life you cannot relinquish the Lordship of Christ to any human lords, authorities, or political leaders.

Prayer: If I must stand today or some day for Christ against all others, Lord, give me courage to endure.

363 REIGNING WITH CHRIST

Then I saw thrones, and seated on them were those to whom judgment was committed. Also I saw the souls of those who had been beheaded for their testimony to Jesus and for the word of God, and who had not worshiped the beast or its image and had not received its mark on their foreheads or their hands. They came to life again, and reigned with Christ a thousand years. The rest of the dead did not come to life again until the thousand years were ended. This is the first resurrection. Blessed and holy is he who shares in the first resurrection! Over such the second death has no power, but they shall be priests of God and of Christ, and they shall reign with him a thousand years. (*Revelation 20:4–6*)

Action Step: Loyal to Christ all the way
The separation Christ brings
The rewards of faithfulness

Action Step: Begin now to speak out for the right as you have studiously and prayerfully discerned it so that you may be able to progressively stand for the right in the face of increasing dangers that could come.

Prayer: What a blessed assurance today, Lord, is the victory of resurrection with Jesus and the courageous saints of the ages.

364 NEW HEAVEN AND EARTH

Then I saw a new heaven and a new earth; for the first heaven and the first earth had passed away, and the sea was no more. And I saw the holy city, new Jerusalem, coming down out of heaven from God, prepared as a bride adorned for her husband; and I heard a loud voice from the throne saying, "Behold, the dwelling of God is with men. He will dwell with them, and they shall be his people, and God himself will be with them; he will wipe away every tear from their eyes, and death shall be no more, neither shall there be mourning nor crying nor pain any more, for the former things have passed away." (*Revelation 21:1–4*)

Key Ideas: God is around us
God is with us
God is for us

Action Step: Make sure your frantic activities and personal investments of resources and energies are linked to the eternal goals of God for His universe.

Prayer: Your goals for our world are so high, Lord, nevertheless and because of this I will keep working today toward both their earthly and heavenly fulfillment.

365 THE CITY OF GOD

And I saw no temple in the city, for its temple is the Lord God the Almighty and the Lamb. And the city has no need of sun or moon to shine upon it, for the glory of God is its light, and its lamp is the Lamb. By its light shall the nations walk; and the kings of the earth shall bring their glory into it, and its gates shall never be shut by day—and there shall be no night there; they shall bring into it the glory and the honor of the nations. But nothing unclean shall enter it, nor any one who practices abomination or falsehood, but only those who are written in the Lamb's book of life. Then he showed me the river of the water of life, bright as crystal, flowing from the throne of God and of the Lamb through the middle of the street of the city; also, on either side of the river, the tree of life with its twelve kinds of fruit, yielding its fruit each month; and the leaves of the tree were for the healing of the nations. (*Revelation 21:22–22:2*)

Key Ideas: Light for the heavenly City
Citizens of the heavenly City
Life for the heavenly City

Action Step: Offer your personal, prayerful, and financial support to the world mission of the Church which recognizes the cultural and spiritual contributions of every nation to the world human family and the family of God.

Prayer: Lord, I will not be discouraged by anything today because of the light of that distant City.

INDEX

NOTE: Numbers refer to daily readings.

A

B

C

D

E

F

G

H

J

K

L

S

T

U

W